British Railw

C000256927

COA
STOCK

FORTY-SIXTH EDITION
2022

The complete guide to all
Locomotive-Hauled Carriages which
operate on the national railway network

Robert Pritchard

SBN 978 1909 431 72 0

© 2021. Platform 5 Publishing Ltd, 52 Broadfield Road, Sheffield, S8 0XJ,
England.

Printed in England by The Lavenham Press, Lavenham, Suffolk.

CONTENTS

Provision of Information 2
Updates 2
Britain's Railway System 3
Introduction 11
1.   British Railways Number Series Coaching Stock 22
2.   High Speed Train Trailer Cars 72
3.   Saloons 86
4.   Pullman Car Company Series 90
5.   Locomotive Support Coaches 93
6.   95xxx & 99xxx Range Number Conversion Table 95
7.   Set Formations 96
8.   Service Stock 98
9.   Coaching Stock Awaiting Disposal 106
10. Codes 108

PROVISION OF INFORMATION

This book has been compiled with care to be as accurate as possible, but some information is not easily available and the publisher cannot be held responsible for any errors or omissions. We would like to thank the companies and individuals who have been helpful in supplying information to us. The authors of this series of books are always pleased to receive notification of any inaccuracies that may be found, to enhance future editions. Please send comments to:

Robert Pritchard, Platform 5 Publishing Ltd, 52 Broadfield Road, Sheffield, S8 0XJ, England.

e-mail: robert.pritchard@platform5.com   **Tel:** 0114 255 2625.

This book is updated to information received by 11 October 2021.

UPDATES

This book is updated to the Stock Changes given in **Today's Railways UK 237** (November 2021). The Platform 5 railway magazine "**Today's Railways UK**" publishes Stock Changes every month to update this book. The magazine also contains news and rolling stock information on the railways of Great Britain and is published on the second Monday of every month. For further details of **Today's Railways UK**, please contact Platform 5 Publishing Ltd or visit our website **www.platform5.com**.

Front cover photograph: West Coast Railway Company maroon-liveried Mark 1 Open First 99371 (3128) is seen at Garsdale on 03/08/21.   **Robert Pritchard**

BRITAIN'S RAILWAY SYSTEM

The structure of Britain's railway system has changed significantly during 2020–21, following the ongoing Covid-19 pandemic which saw passenger numbers drop by around 60–70% across the country. Although passengers started to return in larger numbers during 2021, this original drop in numbers meant that franchises were no longer profitable and the Government was forced to step in and provide financial support to operators. Initially in March 2020 the Transport Secretary suspended rail franchising and operators transitioned to "Emergency Measures Agreements". These EMAs suspended the normal financial agreements, instead transferring all revenue and cost risk to the Government. The existing operators in England all accepted these new arrangements and continued to operate trains (initially with reduced service frequencies) for a small management fee. Similar arrangements were put in place by the Scottish and Welsh Governments for ScotRail, Caledonian Sleeper and Transport for Wales.

The EMAs initially lasted for six months until September 2020, from which time longer "Emergency Recovery Management Agreements" (ERMAs) were put in place. These were similar management contracts which continued to see operators run services for a management fee. Whilst some operators are still running under ERMAs, others are transitioning to new National Rail Contracts (NRCs). During the NRC operators are paid a fixed management fee of around 1.5% for operating services and additional small performance fees if agreed targets are achieved.

In the longer term a new body called Great British Railways will take over the running of the railways and specifically take over Network Rail's responsibilities as well as some functions currently carried out by the Department for Transport and Rail Delivery Group. The franchise model will be changed to one of concessions, although this will take some years to fully implement.

In London and on Merseyside concessions were already in place. These see the operator paid a fee to run the service, usually within tightly specified guidelines. Operators running a concession would not normally take commercial risks, although there are usually penalties and rewards in the contract.

Britain's national railway infrastructure is currently owned by a "not for dividend" company, Network Rail. In 2014 Network Rail was reclassified as a public sector company, being described by the Government as a "public sector arm's-length body of the Department for Transport".

Most stations and maintenance depots are leased to and operated by the Train Operating Companies (TOCs), but some larger stations are controlled by Network Rail. The only exception is the infrastructure on the Isle of Wight: The Island Line franchise uniquely included maintenance of the infrastructure as well as the operation of passenger services. Both the infrastructure and trains are operated by South Western Railway.

Trains are operated by TOCs over Network Rail tracks (the National Network), regulated by access agreements between the parties involved. In general,

TOCs are responsible for the provision and maintenance of the trains and staff necessary for the direct operation of services, whilst Network Rail is responsible for the provision and maintenance of the infrastructure and also for staff to regulate the operation of services.

The Department for Transport (DfT) is the authority for the national network. Transport Scotland oversees the award of the ScotRail and Caledonian Sleeper franchises and in April 2022 will take over the operation of the ScotRail franchise from Abellio. In February 2021 the Welsh Government took over the operation of the Wales & Borders franchise from KeolisAmey.

Each franchise was set up with the right to run specified services within a specified area for a period of time, in return for the right to charge fares and, where appropriate, to receive financial support from the Government. Subsidy was payable in respect of socially necessary services. Service standards are monitored by the DfT throughout the duration of the franchise. Franchisees earned revenue primarily from fares and from subsidy. They generally leased stations from Network Rail and earned rental income by sub-letting parts of them, for example to retailers.

TOC's and open access operator's main costs are the track access charges they pay to Network Rail, the costs of leasing stations and rolling stock and of employing staff. Franchisees may do light maintenance work on rolling stock or contract it out to other companies. Heavy maintenance is normally carried out by the Rolling Stock Leasing Companies, according to contracts.

Note that a railway "reporting period" is four weeks.

DOMESTIC PASSENGER TRAIN OPERATORS

The majority of passenger trains are operated by Train Operating Companies, now supported by the Government through the Emergency Recovery Management Agreements, which have replaced franchises. Some operators are now transitioning to new National Rail Contracts. Caledonian Sleeper and ScotRail are still operating under Emergency Measures Agreements (EMAs). For reference the date of the expiry of the original franchise is also given here (if later than the current ERMA or NRC expiry date).

Name of franchise	Operator	*Trading Name*
Caledonian Sleeper	Serco	**Caledonian Sleeper**

EMA until 31 December 2021; original franchise was until 31 March 2030

The Sleeper franchise started in April 2015 when operation of the ScotRail and ScotRail Sleeper franchises were separated. Abellio won the ScotRail franchise and Serco the Caledonian Sleeper franchise. Caledonian Sleeper operates four trains nightly between London Euston and Scotland using locomotives hired from GBRf. New CAF Mark 5 rolling stock was introduced during 2019.

Chiltern	Arriva (Deutsche Bahn)	**Chiltern Railways**

EMRA until 11 December 2021, the original franchise expiry date

Chiltern Railways operates a frequent service between London Marylebone, Oxford, Banbury and Birmingham Snow Hill, with some peak trains extending to Kidderminster. There are also regular services from Marylebone to Stratford-upon-Avon and to Aylesbury Vale Parkway via Amersham (along the London Underground Metropolitan Line). The fleet consists of DMUs of Classes 165 and 168 plus a number of locomotive-hauled rakes used on some of the Birmingham and Oxford route trains, worked by Class 68s hired from DRS.

Cross Country	Arriva (Deutsche Bahn)	**CrossCountry**

ERMA until 15 October 2023

CrossCountry operates a network of long distance services between Scotland, the North-East of England and Manchester to the South-West of England, Reading, Southampton, Bournemouth and Guildford, centred on Birmingham New Street. These trains are mainly formed of diesel Class 220/221 Voyagers, supplemented by a small number of HSTs on the NE–SW route. Inter-urban services also link Nottingham, Leicester and Stansted Airport with Birmingham and Cardiff. These trains use Class 170 DMUs.

Crossrail	MTR	**TfL Rail**

Concession until 27 May 2023 (with an option to extend the concession by 2 years to May 2025)

This concession started in May 2015. Initially Crossrail took over the Liverpool Street–Shenfield stopping service from Greater Anglia, using a fleet of Class 315 EMUs, with the service branded "TfL Rail". New Class 345 EMUs are being introduced on this route and are also now used between Paddington and Hayes & Harlington, Heathrow Airport and Reading. TfL Rail currently also operates the former Heathrow Connect stopping service that now also uses Class 345s. The opening of Crossrail through central London has been delayed and operation through new tunnels beneath central London, from Shenfield and Abbey Wood in the east to Reading and Heathrow Airport in the west is now expected spring 2022. It will then be branded the "Elizabeth Line".

East Coast	DfT	**London North Eastern Railway**

Operated by DfT's "Operator of Last Resort" until June 2023 (with an option to extend by 2 years to June 2025)

LNER operates frequent long distance trains on the East Coast Main Line between London King's Cross, Leeds, Lincoln, Harrogate, York, Newcastle-upon-Tyne and Edinburgh, with less frequent services to Bradford, Skipton, Hull, Glasgow, Stirling, Aberdeen and Inverness. A new fleet of 65 Hitachi Class 800 and 801 "Azuma" trains have all now been introduced (these are a mix of bi-mode and electric, 5- and 9-car units) and operate the majority of services. A small number of Class 91 + Mark 4 sets have been retained until at least 2023 and are mainly used on Leeds and York services.

East Midlands	Abellio	**East Midlands Railway**

ERMA until 31 March 2022; original franchise was until 21 August 2027

EMR operates a mix of long distance high speed services on the Midland Main Line (MML), from London St Pancras to Sheffield (with one peak-hour train to Leeds), Nottingham (plus peak-hour trains to Lincoln) and Corby, and local and regional services ranging from the long distance Norwich–Liverpool route to Nottingham–Skegness, Nottingham–Mansfield–Worksop, Newark–Matlock and Derby–Crewe. It also operates local services across Lincolnshire. Trains on the MML are worked by a fleet of Class 180 and 222 DMUs, whilst the local and regional fleet consists of DMU Classes 153, 156, 158 and 170. Class 360 EMUs started to operate services on the newly electrified St Pancras–Corby route from May 2021.

East Anglia	Abellio (Netherlands Railways) (60%)/Mitsui Group (40%)	**Greater Anglia**

NRC until 19 September 2024 with option for a 2 year extension; original franchise was until 11 October 2025

Greater Anglia operates main line trains between London Liverpool Street, Ipswich and Norwich and local trains across Norfolk, Suffolk and parts of Cambridgeshire. It also runs local and commuter services into Liverpool Street from the Great Eastern (including Southend, Braintree and Clacton) and West Anglia (including Ely/Cambridge and Stansted Airport) routes. In 2019–20 a new fleet of Stadler EMUs and bi-mode units (Classes 745 and 755) was introduced on the GEML and in East Anglia, replacing older DMUs and loco-hauled trains. Classes 317, 321, 322 and 379 EMUs are still operated out of Liverpool Street and during 2020–22 are being replaced by a large fleet of 133 new Class 720 Aventras.

Essex Thameside — Trenitalia — c2c
NRC until 25 July 2023; original franchise was until 10 November 2029

c2c operates an intensive, principally commuter, service from London Fenchurch Street to Southend and Shoeburyness, via both Upminster and Tilbury. The fleet consists of 74 Class 357 EMUs, with 12 Class 720 Aventras on order.

Great Western — First Group — Great Western Railway
EMA until 25 June 2022; original franchise was until 31 March 2023. New Direct Award being negotiated for a further 3 years + an optional extra 3 years

Great Western Railway operates long distance trains from London Paddington to South Wales, the West Country and Worcester and Hereford. In addition there are frequent trains along the Thames Valley corridor to Newbury/Bedwyn and Oxford, plus local and regional trains throughout the South-West including the Cornish, Devon and Thames Valley branches, the Reading–Gatwick North Downs Line and Cardiff–Portsmouth Harbour and Bristol–Weymouth regional routes. Long distance services are in the hands of a fleet of Class 800/802 bi-mode InterCity Express Trains. DMUs of Classes 165 and 166 are used on the Thames Valley branches and North Downs routes as well as on local services around Bristol and Exeter and across to Cardiff. Class 387 EMUs are used between Paddington, Reading, Didcot Parkway and Newbury. Classes 150, 158, 165 and 166 and a fleet of short 4-car HSTs are used on local and regional trains in the South-West. A small fleet of Class 57s is maintained to work the overnight "Cornish Riviera" Sleeper service between London Paddington and Penzance formed of Mark 3 coaches. In 2021–22 tri-mode Class 769 units will be introduced on some routes around Reading.

London Rail — Arriva (Deutsche Bahn) — London Overground
Concession until 25 May 2024 (with an option to extend the concession by 2 years to May 2026)

London Overground operates services on the Richmond–Stratford North London Line and the Willesden Junction–Clapham Junction West London Line, plus the East London Line from Highbury & Islington to New Cross and New Cross Gate, with extensions to Clapham Junction (via Denmark Hill), Crystal Palace and West Croydon. It also runs services from London Euston to Watford Junction. All these use Class 378 EMUs, with new Class 710s also recently introduced onto the Watford Junction route. Class 710s also operate services on the Gospel Oak–Barking line. London Overground also operates some suburban services from London Liverpool Street — to Chingford, Enfield Town and Cheshunt. These services all use Class 710s, with one unit also used on the Romford–Upminster shuttle.

Merseyrail Electrics — Serco (50%)/Abellio (Netherlands Railways) (50%) — Merseyrail
Concession until 22 July 2028. Under the control of Merseytravel PTE instead of the DfT
Due to be reviewed every five years to fit in with the Merseyside Local Transport Plan

Merseyrail operates services between Liverpool and Southport, Ormskirk, Kirkby, Hunts Cross, New Brighton, West Kirby, Chester and Ellesmere Port, using Class 507 and 508 EMUs. A new fleet of Class 777 EMUs will be introduced in 2022–23.

Northern

DfT   **Northern**

Operated by DfT's "Operator of Last Resort" until further notice

Northern operates a range of inter-urban, commuter and rural services throughout the North of England, including those around the cities of Leeds, Manchester, Sheffield, Liverpool and Newcastle. The network extends from Chathill in the north to Nottingham in the south, and Cleethorpes in the east to St Bees in the west. Long distance services include Leeds–Carlisle, Morpeth–Carlisle and York–Blackpool North. The operator uses a large fleet of DMUs of Classes 150, 153, 155, 156, 158, 170 and 195 plus EMU Classes 319, 323, 331 and 333. The new fleets of DMUs (Class 195) and EMUs (Class 331) have now been introduced as a number of routes, and were followed by Class 769 bi-mode diesel electric units (converted from Class 319s) in 2021.

ScotRail

Abellio (Netherlands Railways)   **ScotRail**

EMA until 31 December 2021; original franchise was until 31 March 2022. From 1 April 2022 the Scottish Government will take over the operation of the franchise.

ScotRail provides almost all passenger services within Scotland and also trains from Glasgow to Carlisle via Dumfries, some of which extend to Newcastle-upon-Tyne (jointly operated with Northern). The company operates a large fleet of DMUs of Classes 156, 158 and 170 and EMU Classes 318, 320, 334, 380 and 385. A fleet of 25 refurbished HSTs are being introduced onto InterCity services between Edinburgh/Glasgow and Aberdeen and Inverness and also between Inverness and Aberdeen. In 2021 five Class 153s were also introduced on the West Highland Line (Oban line) to provide more capacity and space for bikes and other luggage.

South Eastern

DfT   **Southeastern**

Operated by DfT's "Operator of Last Resort" from 17 October 2021 until further notice. Govia was stripped of the franchise following a breach of its franchise commitment.

Southeastern operates all services in the south-east London suburbs, the whole of Kent and part of Sussex, which are primarily commuter services to London. It also operates domestic High Speed trains on HS1 from London St Pancras to Ashford, Ramsgate, Dover and Faversham with additional peak services on other routes. EMUs of Classes 375, 376, 377, 465 and 466 are used, along with Class 395s on the High Speed trains. In 2021–22 the 30 Class 707 EMUs, sub-leased from South Western Railway, are also being introduced.

South Western

First Group (70%)/MTR (30%)   **South Western Railway**

JRC until 30 May 2023 with option for a 2 year extension; original franchise ran until 17 August 2024

South Western Railway operates trains from London Waterloo to destinations across the south and South-West including Woking, Basingstoke, Southampton, Portsmouth, Salisbury, Exeter, Reading and Weymouth, as well as suburban services from Waterloo. SWR also runs services between Ryde and Shanklin on the Isle of Wight, from November 2021 using a fleet of five third rail Vivarail Class 484 units (converted former LU D78 stock). The rest of the fleet consists of DMU Classes 158 and 159 and EMU Classes 444, 450, 455, 456, 458 and 707. A new fleet of Bombardier Class 701s are being delivered to replace Classes 455, 456 and 707 in 2021–22.

Thameslink, Southern & Great Northern (TSGN)

Govia (Go-Ahead/Keolis)   **Govia Thameslink Railway**

RMA until 31 March 2022

TSGN is the largest operator in Great Britain (the former Southern franchise was combined with Thameslink/Great Northern in 2015). GTR uses four brands: "Thameslink" for trains between Cambridge North, Peterborough, Bedford and Rainham, Sevenoaks, East Grinstead,

Brighton, Littlehampton and Horsham via central London and also on the Sutton/Wimbledon loop using Class 700 EMUs. "Great Northern" comprises services from London King's Cross and Moorgate to Welwyn Garden City, Hertford North, Peterborough, Cambridge and King's Lynn using Class 387 and 717 EMUs. "Southern" operates predominantly commuter services between London, Surrey and Sussex and "metro" services in South London, as well as services along the south Coast between Southampton, Brighton, Hastings and Ashford, plus the cross-London service from South Croydon to Milton Keynes. Class 171 DMUs are used on Ashford–Eastbourne and London Bridge–Uckfield services, whilst all other services are in the hands of Class 313, 377, 455 and 700 EMUs. Finally, Gatwick Express operates non-stop trains between London Victoria, Gatwick Airport and Brighton using Class 387/2 EMUs.

Trans-Pennine Express   First Group   **TransPennine Express**
NRC until 30 May 2023 with option for a 2 year extension

TransPennine Express operates predominantly long distance inter-urban services linking major cities across the North of England, along with Edinburgh and Glasgow in Scotland. The main services are Manchester Airport–Redcar Central, Manchester Piccadilly–Hull, Liverpool–York–Scarborough and Liverpool–Newcastle/Edinburgh along the North Trans-Pennine route via Huddersfield, Leeds and York, and Manchester Piccadilly–Cleethorpes along the South Trans-Pennine route via Sheffield. TPE also operates Manchester Airport–Edinburgh/Glasgow and Liverpool–Glasgow. The fleet consists of Class 185 DMUs, plus three new fleets: Class 68s+Mark 5A sets being used, or to be used, on Liverpool–Scarborough and Manchester Airport–Redcar Central, Class 397s used on Manchester Airport/Liverpool–Scotland and Class 802 bi-mode units used on Liverpool–Newcastle/Edinburgh.

Wales & Borders   Welsh Government   **Transport for Wales**
From 7 February 2021 the Welsh Government will take direct control of rail service operation. Infrastructure management is continued to be managed by KeolisAmey.

Transport for Wales was procured by the Welsh Government and operates a mix of long distance, regional and local services throughout Wales, including the Valley Lines network of lines around Cardiff, and also through services to the English border counties and to Manchester and Birmingham. The fleet consists of DMUs of Classes 150, 153, 158, 170 and 175 and three locomotive-hauled Mark 4 sets hauled by Class 67s on the Cardiff–Holyhead route. Rebuilt Class 230 D-Trains will be introduced on the Wrexham–Bidston line in 2021–22 and new Stadler and CAF fleets will be introduced across other routes from 2022.

West Coast Partnership   First Group (70%)/Trenitalia (30%)   **Avanti West Coast**
ERMA until 15 October 2022; original franchise ran until 31 March 2031. New Direct Award being negotiated for upto 10 years

Avanti West Coast operates long distance services along the West Coast Main Line from London Euston to Birmingham/Wolverhampton, Manchester, Liverpool, Blackpool North and Glasgow using Class 390 Pendolino EMUs. It also operates Class 221 Voyagers on the Euston–Chester–Holyhead route and a small number of trains from Wolverhampton to Shrewsbury and to Wrexham, whilst a mix of Class 221s and 390s are used on the Euston–Birmingham–Glasgow/Edinburgh route.

West Midlands Trains   Abellio (70%)/JR East (15%)/Mitsui (15%)   **West Midlands Railway**
                                                       London Northwestern
NRC until 19 September 2024 with option for a 2 year extension; original franchise ran until 31 March 2026

West Midlands Trains operates services under two brand names. West Midlands Railway trains are local and regional services around Birmingham, including to Stratford-upon-Avon

Worcester, Hereford, Redditch, Rugeley and Shrewsbury. WMR is managed by a consortium of 16 councils and the Department for Transport. London Northwestern is the brand used for long distance and regional services from London Euston to Northampton and Birmingham/Crewe and also between Birmingham and Liverpool, Bedford–Bletchley and Watford Junction–St Albans Abbey. The fleet consists of DMU Classes 139, 170 and 172 and EMU Classes 319, 323 and 350. Class 230 D-Trains were introduced onto the Bedford–Bletchley route in 2019 and a new fleet CAF Class 196 DMUs and Bombardier Class 730 EMUs will be introduced on a number of routes from 2022.

NON-FRANCHISED SERVICES

The following operators run non-franchised, or "open access" services (* special seasonal services):

Operator	Trading Name	Route
Heathrow Airport Holdings	Heathrow Express	London Paddington–Heathrow Airport

Heathrow Express is a frequent express passenger service between London Paddington and Heathrow Airport using a sub-fleet of Great Western Railway Class 387 EMUs (now operated jointly with GWR as part of its franchise).

Hull Trains (part of First)	Hull Trains	London King's Cross–Hull

Hull Trains operates six trains a day on weekdays from Hull to London King's Cross via the East Coast Main Line. New bi-mode Class 802s were introduced in 2019–20, replacing the Class 180 DMUs. Two trains in each direction start back from and extend to Beverley.

Grand Central (part of Arriva)	Grand Central	London King's Cross–Sunderland/Bradford Interchange

Grand Central operates four trains a day from Sunderland and four from Bradford Interchange to London King's Cross using Class 180 DMUs.

Locomotive Services (TOC)	Locomotive Services	

Locomotive Services runs various excursions across the network using diesel, electric and steam locomotives operating under the brands Saphos Trains (principally steam-hauled trips), Statesman Rail (diesel-locomotive hauled trips and land cruises), Rail Charter Services (regular seasonal HSTs over the Settle & Carlisle Line), Midland Pullman (HST tours) and Intercity (electric locomotive-hauled tours).

First East Coast	Lumo	London King's Cross–Edinburgh

Lumo started operating services from London to Edinburgh via the East Coast Main Line in October 2021 and from early 2022 will be running five trains per day using new electric Class 803 units.

North Yorkshire Moors Railway Enterprises	North Yorkshire Moors Railway	Pickering–Grosmont–Whitby/Battersby, Sheringham–Cromer*

The North Yorkshire Moors Railway operates services on the national network between Grosmont and Whitby or Grosmont and Battersby as an extension of its Pickering–Grosmont services and also operates services between Sheringham and Cromer on behalf of the North Norfolk Railway.

South Yorkshire Supertram	Stagecoach Supertram	Meadowhall South–Rotherham Parkgate

South Yorkshire Supertram holds a passenger licence to allow the operation of the pilot tram-train service linking Sheffield city centre with Rotherham Central and Rotherham Parkgate.

Tyne & Wear PTE	Tyne & Wear Metro	Pelaw–Sunderland

Tyne & Wear Passenger Transport Executive holds a passenger license to allow the operation of its Metro service over Network Rail tracks between Pelaw and Sunderland.

Vintage Trains	Vintage Trains	Birmingham Snow Hill–Stratford-upon-Avon*

Vintage Trains operates steam-hauled services on a seasonal basis.

West Coast Railway Company	West Coast Railway Company	Fort William–Mallaig* York–Settle–Carlisle* Carnforth–York–Scarborough*

WCRC operates steam-hauled services on these routes on a seasonal basis and a range of other excursions across the network.

INTERNATIONAL PASSENGER OPERATORS

Eurostar International operates passenger services between London St Pancras and mainland Europe. The company, established in 2010, is jointly owned by SNCF (the national operator of France): 55%, SNCB (the national operator of Belgium): 5% and Patina Rail: 40%. Patina Rail is made up of Canadian-based Caisse de dépôt et placement du Québec (CDPG) and UK-based Hermes Infrastructure (owning 30% and 10% respectively). This 40% was previously owned by the UK Government until it was sold in 2015.

In addition, a service for the conveyance of accompanied road vehicles through the Channel Tunnel is provided by the tunnel operating company, Eurotunnel. All Eurotunnel services are operated in top-and-tail mode by the powerful Class 9 Bo-Bo-Bo locomotives.

FREIGHT TRAIN OPERATORS

The following operators operate freight services or empty passenger stock workings under "open access" arrangements:

Colas Rail
DB Cargo (UK)
Devon & Cornwall Railways
Direct Rail Services
Freightliner
GB Railfreight
LORAM (UK)
Rail Operations Group
West Coast Railway Company

In addition, Amey, Balfour Beatty Rail, Harsco Rail, Swietelsky Babcock Rail (SB Rail) and VolkerRail operate trains formed of On-Track Machines.

INTRODUCTION

This book contains details of all locomotive-hauled or propelled coaching stock, often referred to as carriages, which can run on Britain's national railway network.

The number of locomotive-hauled or propelled carriages in use on the national railway network is much fewer than was once the case. Those that remain fall into two distinct groups.

Firstly, there are those used by franchised and open access operators for regular timetabled services. Most of these are formed in fixed or semi-fixed formations with either locomotives or a locomotive and Driving Brake Carriage at either end which allows for push-pull operation. There are also a small number of mainly overnight trains with variable formations that use conventional locomotive haulage.

Secondly there are those used for what can best be described as excursion trains. These include a wide range of carriage types ranging from luxurious saloons to those more suited to the "bucket and spade" seaside type of excursion. These are formed into sets to suit the requirements of the day. From time to time some see limited use with franchised and open access operators to cover for stock shortages and times of exceptional demand such as major sporting events.

In addition, there remain a small number of carriages referred to as "Service Stock" which are used internally within the railway industry and are not used to convey passengers.

FRANCHISED & OPEN ACCESS OPERATORS

For each operator regularly using locomotive-hauled carriages brief details are given here of the sphere of operation. For details of operators using HSTs see Section 2.

Caledonian Sleeper

This franchise, operated by Serco, started in 2015 when the Anglo-Scottish Sleeper operation was split from the ScotRail franchise. Caledonian Sleeper operates seating and sleeping car services between London Euston and Scotland using sets of new CAF Mark 5 Sleeping Cars and seated carriages.

GBRf is contracted to supply the motive power for the Sleepers. Class 92s are used between London Euston and Edinburgh/Glasgow Central and rebuilt Class 73/9s between Edinburgh and Inverness, Aberdeen and Fort William.

Chiltern Railways

Chiltern operates four sets of Mark 3 carriages hauled by DRS Class 68 locomotives on its Mainline services between London Marylebone and Birmingham Moor Street/Kidderminster (plus one train to Oxford). Trains operate as push-pull sets.

Great Western Railway
The "Night Riviera" seating and sleeping car service between London Paddington and Penzance uses sets of Mark 3 carriages hauled by Class 57/6 locomotives.

London North Eastern Railway
LNER has retained eight rakes of Mark 4 carriages and these are hauled by Class 91 locomotives in push-pull formation on a limited number of InterCity services between London King's Cross and Leeds or York. All other services on the East Coast Main Line are now in the hands of LNER's fleet of 65 "Azuma" bi-mode units.

North Yorkshire Moors Railway
In addition to operating the North Yorkshire Moors Railway between Pickering and Grosmont the company operates through services to Whitby and occasionally Battersby. A fleet of Mark 1 passenger carriages and Pullman Cars are used for these services. It also operates the "North Norfolkman" services on behalf of the North Norfolk Railway between Sheringham and Cromer.

TransPennine Express
TPE has 13 sets of new CAF Mark 5A coaches that were originally due to enter service in 2019 but due to teething problems and delays with crew training now not due to enter full service until 2022. The sets are being used on some services on the Liverpool–Scarborough route and they are also due to be used on the Manchester Airport–Redcar route. They are operated using DRS Class 68s in push-pull mode.

Transport for Wales
TfW ceased using its Mark 3 rakes during the Covid-19 lockdown in March 2020. It has taken on lease three shortened rakes of ex-LNER Mark 4s and these were introduced in spring 2021 on the Cardiff–Holyhead route, in push-pull mode with Class 67s. TfW has also purchased an additional four Mark 4 rakes that will be used on the Manchester–Swansea route from late 2022.

West Coast Railway Company
WCRC operates two sets of Mark 1/2 carriages on its regular steam-hauled "Jacobite" trains between Fort William and Mallaig. These trains normally operate between late April and late October.

EXCURSION TRAIN OPERATORS

Usually, three types of companies will be involved in the operation of an excursion train. There will be the promoter, the rolling stock provider and the train operator. In many cases two or more of these roles may be undertaken by the same or associated companies. Only a small number of Train Operating Companies facilitate the operation of excursion trains. This takes various forms ranging from the complete package of providing and operating the train, through offering a "hook up and haul" service, to operating the train for a third-party rolling stock custodian.

DB Cargo UK

DBC currently operates its own luxurious train of Mark 3 carriages, called the Company Train. It also offers a hook up and haul service and regularly operates the Royal Train and the Belmond British Pullman as well as trains for Riviera Trains and their client promoters.

Direct Rail Services

DRS has a fleet of Mark 2 carriages originally intended for use on excursion trains, that until spring 2020 were hired to ScotRail. The company also offers a hook up and haul service for Riviera Trains and its client promoters.

GB Railfreight

GBRf initially operated excursion trains using the preserved Class 201 "Hastings" DEMU. It now also operates a small number of company excursions using hired-in carriages. The company also offers a hook up and haul service operating the Royal Scotsman luxury train, as well as trains for Riviera Trains and its client promoters.

Locomotive Services

This vertically integrated company gained a license in 2017. From its base at Crewe excursion trains are operated across the country using its increasingly varied fleet of steam, diesel and electric locomotives and Mark 1/2/3 carriages, and from 2020 the "Midland Pullman" HST set.

Rail Operations Group

This company has operated a small number of excursion trains using hired in carriages. It also offers a hook up and haul service.

Vintage Trains

This vertically integrated company gained a licence in 2018. From its base at Tyseley it operates the "Shakespeare Express" steam service between Birmingham and Stratford-upon-Avon. It also operates excursions using its fleet of steam and diesel locomotives and Mark 1/2 carriages and Pullman cars.

West Coast Railway Company

This vertically integrated company has its own fleet of steam and diesel locomotives as well as a full range of different carriage types. It operates its own regular trains, including the luxury Northern Belle, the "Jacobite" steam service between Fort William and Mallaig, the "Dalesman" steam and diesel services over the Settle & Carlisle route and numerous excursion trains for itself and client promoters. In addition, it offers a hook up and haul service operating trains for companies such as The Princess Royal Locomotive Trust and the Scottish Railway Preservation Society.

LAYOUT OF INFORMATION

Carriages are listed in numerical order of painted number in batches according to type.

Where a carriage has been renumbered, the former number is shown in parentheses. If a carriage has been renumbered more than once, the original number is shown first, followed by the most recent previous number.

Each carriage entry is laid out as in the following example (previous number(s) column may be omitted where not applicable):

No.	Prev. No.	Notes	Livery	Owner	Operator	Depot/Location
82301	(82117)	g	**CM**	AV	CR	AL

Codes: Codes are used to denote the livery, owner, operator and depot/location of each carriage. Details of codes used can be found in Section 10 of this book.

The owner is the responsible custodian of the carriage and this may not always be the legal owner. Actual ownership can be very complicated. Some vehicles are owned by finance/leasing companies. Others are owned by subsidiary companies of a holding company or by an associate company of the responsible custodian or operator.

The operator is the organisation which facilitates the use of the carriage and may not be the actual train operating company which runs the train. If no operator is shown the carriage is considered to be not in use.

The depot is the facility primarily responsible for the carriages maintenance. Light maintenance and heavy overhauls may be carried out elsewhere.

The location is where carriages not in use are currently being kept or are stored.

GENERAL INFORMATION

CLASSIFICATION AND NUMBERING

Seven different numbering systems were in use on British Rail. These were the British Rail series, the four pre-nationalisation companies' series', the Pullman Car Company's series and the UIC (International Union of Railways) series. In this book BR number series carriages and former Pullman Car Company series are listed separately. There is also a separate listing of "Saloon" type carriages, that includes pre-nationalisation survivors, which are permitted to run on the national railway system, Locomotive Support Carriages and Service Stock. Please note the Mark 2 Pullman carriages were ordered after the Pullman Car Company had been nationalised and are therefore numbered in the British Rail series. The new CAF Mark 5 carriages have been allocated numbers in the British Rail series.

Also listed separately are the British Rail and Pullman Car Company number series carriages used on North Yorkshire Moors Railway and North Norfolk Railway services on very limited parts of the national railway network. This is due to their very restricted sphere of operation.

The BR number series grouped carriages of a particular type together in chronological order. Major modifications affecting type of accommodation resulted in renumbering into a more appropriate or new number series. Since privatisation such renumbering has not always taken place resulting in renumbering which has been more haphazard and greater variations within numbering groups.

With the introduction of the TOPS numbering system, coaching stock (including multiple unit vehicles) retained their original BR number unless this conflicted with a locomotive number. Carriages can be one–five digits, although no one or two-digit examples remain in use on the national network. BR generally numbered "Service Stock" in a six-digit wagon number series.

UNITS OF MEASUREMENT

All dimensions and weights are quoted for carriages in an "as new" condition or after a major modification, such as fitting with new bogies etc. Dimensions are quoted in the order length x width. Lengths quoted are over buffers or couplers as appropriate. All widths quoted are maxima. All weights are shown as metric tonnes (t = tonnes).

DIMENSIONS

Carriage lengths are summarised as follows:

Mark 1: 19.35 m or 17.37 m.   **Mark 4:** 23.00 m.
Mark 2: 19.66 m.   **Mark 5:** 22.20 m.
Mark 3: 23.00 m.   **Mark 5A:** 22.20–22.37 m.
Mark 3 HST: 23.00 m.

DETAILED INFORMATION & CODES

Under each type heading, the following details are shown:

* "Mark" of carriage (see below).
* Descriptive text.
* Number of First Class seats, Standard Class seats, lavatory
  compartments and wheelchair spaces shown as F/S nT nW respectively.
  A number in brackets indicates tip-up seats (in addition to the regular
  seats).
* Bogie type (see below).
* Additional features.
* ETS Index.
* Weight: All weights are shown as metric tonnes.

BOGIE TYPES

Gresley. LNER design of bogie first used in the "Gresley" era. Used by BR on some Mark 1 catering carriages. Now used for some saloons.

BR Mark 1 (BR1). Double bolster leaf spring bogie. Generally 90 mph, but Mark 1 bogies may be permitted to run at 100 mph with special maintenance. Weight: 6.1 t.

BR Mark 2 (BR2). Single bolster leaf-spring bogie used on certain types of non-passenger stock and suburban stock (all now withdrawn). Weight: 5.3 t.

COMMONWEALTH (C). Heavy, cast steel coil spring bogie. 100 mph. Weight: 6.75 t.

B4. Coil spring fabricated bogie. Generally 100 mph, but B4 bogies may be permitted to run at 110 mph with special maintenance. Weight: 5.2 t.

B5. Heavy duty version of B4. 100 mph. Weight: 5.3 t.

B5 (SR). A bogie originally used on Southern Region EMUs, similar in design to B5. Now also used on locomotive-hauled carriages. 100 mph.

BT10. A fabricated bogie designed for 125 mph. Air suspension.

T4. A 125 mph bogie designed by BREL (now Bombardier Transportation).

BT41. Fitted to Mark 4 carriages, designed by SIG in Switzerland. At present limited to 125 mph, but designed for 140 mph.

CAF. Fitted to CAF Mark 5 and Mark 5A carriages.

BRAKES

Air braking is now standard on British main line trains. Carriages with other equipment are denoted:

Air braked, through vacuum pipe.
Vacuum braked.
Dual braked (air and vacuum).

HEATING & VENTILATION

Electric heating and ventilation is now standard on British main-line trains. Certain carriages for use on excursion services may also have steam heating facilities, or be steam heated only. All carriages used on North Yorkshire Moors Railway and North Norfolk Railway trains have steam heating.

NOTES ON ELECTRIC TRAIN SUPPLY

The sum of ETS indices in a train must be not more than the ETS index of the locomotive or generator van. The normal voltage on British trains is 1000 V. Suffix "X" denotes 600 amp wiring instead of 400 amp. Trains whose ETS index is higher than 66 must be formed completely of 600 amp wired stock. Class 33 and 73/1 locomotives cannot provide a suitable electric train supply for Mark 2D, Mark 2E, Mark 2F, Mark 3, Mark 3A, Mark 3B or Mark 4 carriages. Class 55 locomotives provide an ETS directly from one of their traction generators into the train line. Consequently voltage fluctuations can result in motor-alternator flashover. Thus these locomotives are not suitable for use with Mark 2D, Mark 2E, Mark 2F, Mark 3, Mark 3A, Mark 3B or Mark 4 carriages unless modified motor-alternators are fitted. Such motor alternators were fitted to Mark 2D and 2F carriages used on the East Coast Main Line, but few remain fitted.

PUBLIC ADDRESS

It is assumed all carriages are now fitted with public address equipment, although certain stored carriages may not have this feature. In addition, it is assumed all carriages with a conductor's compartment have public address transmission facilities, as have catering carriages.

COOKING EQUIPMENT

It is assumed that Mark 1 catering carriages have gas powered cooking equipment, whilst Mark 2, 3 and 4 catering carriages have electric powered cooking equipment unless stated otherwise.

ADDITIONAL FEATURE CODES

(+4)	Indicates tip-up seats in that carriage (in addition to the fixed seats).
d	Central Door Locking.
dg	Driver–Guard communication equipment.
f	Facelifted or fluorescent lighting.
h	"High density" seating
k	Composition brake blocks (instead of cast iron).
n	Day/night lighting.
pg	Public address transmission and driver-guard communication.
pt	Public address transmission facility.
q	Catering staff to shore telephone.
T	Toilet
TD	A universal access toilet suitable for use by person of reduced mobility
w	Wheelchair space.

BUILD DETAILS

Lot Numbers
Vehicles ordered under the auspices of BR were allocated a lot (batch) number when ordered and these are quoted in class headings and sub-headings.

Builders
These are shown in class headings, the following designations being used

Ashford	BR, Ashford Works.
BRCW	Birmingham Railway Carriage & Wagon Company Smethwick, Birmingham.
BREL Derby	BREL, Derby Carriage Works (later ABB/Adtranz Bombardier Transportation Derby, now Alstom Derby).
Charles Roberts	Charles Roberts & Company, Horbury, Wakefield (later Bombardier Transportation).
Cravens	Cravens, Sheffield.
Derby	BR, Derby Carriage Works (later BREL Derby, then ABB Adtranz/Bombardier Transportation Derby, now Alstom Derby).
Doncaster	BR, Doncaster Works (later BREL Doncaster, the BRML Doncaster, then ABB/Adtranz Doncaster, the Bombardier).
Eastleigh	BR, Eastleigh Works (later BREL Eastleigh, then Wessex Traincare, and Alstom Eastleigh, now Arlington Fleet Services).
Glasgow	BR Springburn Works, Glasgow (now closed).
Gloucester	The Gloucester Railway Carriage & Wagon Co.
Hunslet-Barclay	Hunslet Barclay, Kilmarnock Works (later Wabtec Rail Scotland, now Brodies).
Metro-Cammell	Metropolitan-Cammell, Saltley, Birmingham (later GEC Alsthom Birmingham, then Alstom Birmingham).
Pressed Steel	Pressed Steel, Linwood.

Swindon	BR Swindon Works.
Wolverton	BR Wolverton Works (later BREL Wolverton then Railcare, Wolverton, then Alstom, Wolverton now Gemini Rail Group).
York	BR, York Carriage Works (later BREL York, then ABB York).

Information on sub-contracting works which built parts of vehicles eg the underframes etc is not shown. In addition to the above, certain vintage Pullman cars were built or rebuilt at the following works:

Metropolitan Carriage & Wagon Company, Birmingham (later Alstom).
Midland Carriage & Wagon Company, Birmingham.
Pullman Car Company, Preston Park, Brighton.
Conversions have also been carried out at the Railway Technical Centre, Derby, LNWR, Crewe and Blakes Fabrications, Edinburgh.

ABBREVIATIONS

The following abbreviations are used in class headings and also throughout this publication:

BR	British Railways.
DB	Deutsche Bahn
DEMU	Diesel Electric Multiple Unit.
DMU	Diesel Multiple Unit (general term).
EMU	Electric Multiple Unit.
ETH	Electric Train Heating
ETS	Electric Train Supply
ft	feet
GWR	Great Western Railway
kN	kilonewtons.
km/h	kilometres per hour.
kW	kilowatts.
LT	London Transport.
LUL	London Underground Limited.
m	metres.
mph	miles per hour.
SR	BR Southern Region
t	tonnes

THE DEVELOPMENT OF BR STANDARD COACHES

Mark 1

The standard BR coach built from 1951 to 1963 was the Mark 1. This type features a separate underframe and body. The underframe is normally 64 ft 6 in long, but certain vehicles were built on shorter (57 ft) frames. Tungsten lighting was standard and until 1961, BR Mark 1 bogies were generally provided. In 1959 Lot No. 30525 (Open Standard) appeared with fluorescent lighting and melamine interior panels, and from 1961 onwards Commonwealth bogies were fitted in an attempt to improve the quality of ride which became very poor when the tyre profiles on the wheels of the BR1 bogies became worn. Later batches of Open Standard and Open Brake Standard retained the features of Lot No. 30525, but compartment vehicles – whilst utilising melamine panelling in Standard Class – still retained tungsten lighting. Wooden interior finish was retained in First Class vehicles where the only change was to fluorescent lighting in open vehicles (except Lot No. 30648, which had tungsten lighting). In later years many Mark 1 coaches had BR 1 bogies replaced by B4. More recently a small number of carriages have had BR1 bogies replaced with Commonwealth bogies.

XP64

In 1964, a new prototype train was introduced. Known as "XP64", it featured new seat designs, pressure heating & ventilation, aluminium compartment doors and corridor partitions, foot pedal operated toilets and B4 bogies. The vehicles were built on standard Mark 1 underframes. Folding exterior doors were fitted, but these proved troublesome and were later replaced with hinged doors. All XP64 coaches have been withdrawn, but some have been preserved.

Mark 2

The prototype Mark 2 vehicle (W13252) was produced in 1963. This was a Corridor First of semi-integral construction and had pressure heating & ventilation, tungsten lighting, and was mounted on B4 bogies. This vehicle has now been preserved at the Mid Norfolk Railway. The production build was similar, but wider windows were used. The Open Standard vehicles used a new seat design similar to that in the XP64 and fluorescent lighting was provided. Interior finish reverted to wood. Mark 2 vehicles were built from 1964–66.

Mark 2A–2C

The Mark 2A design, built 1967–68, incorporated the remainder of the features first used in the XP64 coaches, ie foot pedal operated toilets (except Open Brake Standard), new First Class seat design, aluminium compartment doors and partitions together with fluorescent lighting in first class compartments. Folding gangway doors (lime green coloured) were used instead of the traditional one-piece variety.

Mark 2B coaches had wide wrap around doors at vehicle ends, no centre doors and a slightly longer body. In Standard Class there was one toilet at each end instead of two at one end as previously. The folding gangway doors were red.

Mark 2C coaches had a lowered ceiling with twin strips of fluorescent lighting and ducting for air conditioning, but air conditioning was never fitted.

Mark 2D–2F

These vehicles were fitted with air conditioning. They had no opening top-lights in saloon windows, which were shallower than previous ones.

Mark 2E vehicles had smaller toilets with luggage racks opposite. The folding gangway doors were fawn coloured.

Mark 2F vehicles had a modified air conditioning system, plastic interior panels and InterCity 70 type seats.

Mark 3

The Mark 3 design has BT10 bogies, is 75 ft (23 m) long and is of fully integral construction with InterCity 70 type seats. Gangway doors were yellow (red in Kitchen Buffet First) when new, although these were changed on refurbishment. Locomotive-hauled coaches are classified Mark 3A, Mark 3 being reserved for HST trailers. A new batch of Open First and Open Brake First, classified Mark 3B, was built in 1985 with Advanced Passenger Train-style seating and revised lighting. The last vehicles in the Mark 3 series were the driving brake vans ("Driving Van Trailers") built for West Coast Main Line services but now mostly withdrawn.

A number of Mark 3 vehicles were converted for use as HST trailers with CrossCountry, Grand Central and Great Western Railway.

Mark 4

The Mark 4 design was built by Metro-Cammell for use on the East Coast Main Line after electrification and featured a body profile suitable for tilting trains, although tilt is not fitted, and is not intended to be. This design is suitable for 140 mph running, although is restricted to 125 mph because the signalling system on the route is not suitable for the higher speed. The bogies for these coaches were built by SIG in Switzerland and are designated BT41. Power operated sliding plug exterior doors are standard. All Mark 4s were rebuilt with completely new interiors in 2003–05 for GNER and referred to as "Mallard" stock. These rakes generally run in fixed formations eight are still operated by London North Eastern Railway and three shorter sets (with four more to come) by Transport for Wales.

New CAF carriages have recently been introduced by Caledonian Sleeper and TransPennine Express. CAF has designated them "Mark 5" and "Mark 5A" but it should be emphasised that these are not a development of the BR standard coach.

1. BRITISH RAILWAYS NUMBER SERIES COACHING STOCK

KITCHEN FIRST

Mark 1. Spent most of its life as a Royal Train vehicle and was numbered 2907 for a time. 24/–. B5 bogies. ETS 2.

Lot No. 30633 Swindon 1961. 41 t.

325   **VN**   WC   *WC*   CS   DUART

PULLMAN KITCHEN

Mark 2. Pressure Ventilated. Built with First Class seating but this has been replaced with a servery area. Gas cooking. 2T. B5 bogies. ETS 6.

Lot No. 30755 Derby 1966. 40 t.

504   **PC**   WC   *WC*   CS   ULLSWATER
506   **PC**   WC   *WC*   CS   WINDERMERE

PULLMAN OPEN FIRST

Mark 2. Pressure Ventilated. 36/–. 2T. B4 bogies. ETS 5.

Lot No. 30754 Derby 1966. 35 t.

Non-standard livery: 546 Maroon & beige.

546   **0**   WC   CS   CITY OF MANCHESTER
548   **PC**   WC   *WC*   CS   GRASMERE
549   **PC**   WC   *WC*   CS   BASSENTHWAITE
550   **PC**   WC   *WC*   CS   RYDAL WATER
551   **PC**   WC   *WC*   CS   BUTTERMERE
552   **PC**   WC   *WC*   CS   ENNERDALE WATER
553   **PC**   WC   *WC*   CS   CRUMMOCK WATER

PULLMAN OPEN BRAKE FIRST

Mark 2. Pressure Ventilated. 30/–. 2T. B4 bogies. ETS 4.

Lot No. 30753 Derby 1966. 35 t.

586   **PC**   WC   *WC*   CS   DERWENTWATER

BUFFET FIRST

Mark 2F. Air conditioned. Converted 1988–89/91 at BREL, Derby from Mark 2F Open Firsts. 1200/03/11/20/21 have Stones equipment, others have Temperature Ltd. 25/– 1T 1W. B4 bogies. d. ETS 6X.

200/03/11/20. Lot No. 30845 Derby 1973. 33 t.
207/10/12/21. Lot No. 30859 Derby 1973–74. 33 t.

200	(3287, 6459)	**BG**	RV	*RV*	BU
203	(3291)	**CC**	LS	*LS*	CL
207	(3328, 6422)	**V**	WC		CS
210	(3405, 6462)	**FS**	ER		YA
211	(3305)	**PC**	LS	*LS*	CL	SNAEFELL
212	(3427, 6453)	**BG**	RV	*RV*	BU
220	(3315, 6432)	**FS**	ER		WO
221	(3371)	**IC**	WC		CS

KITCHEN WITH BAR

Mark 1. Built with no seats but three Pullman-style seats now fitted in bar area. B5 bogies. ETS 1.

Lot No. 30624 Cravens 1960–61. 41 t.

566	**VN**	WC	*WC*	CS	CAERDYDD

KITCHEN BUFFET UNCLASSIFIED

Mark 1. Built with 23 loose chairs. All remaining vehicles were refurbished with 23 fixed polypropylene chairs and fluorescent lighting. 1683/91 were further refurbished with 21 chairs, wheelchair space and carpets. ETS 2 (* 2X).

Now used on excursion trains with the seating area adapted to various uses including servery and food preparation areas, with some or all seating removed.

651–91. Lot No. 30628 Pressed Steel 1960–61. Commonwealth bogies. 39 t.
730. Lot No. 30512 BRCW 1960–61. B5 bogies. 37 t.

651		**CC**	RV	*RV*	ZG	1683	**RB**	RV		BU
657		**BG**	RV	*RV*	BU	1691	**BG**	RV	*RV*	BU
666	x	**M**	RP	*WC*	CS	1730	x	**CC**	SP	*SP*	BO
671	x*	**CH**	RV	*RV*	ZG					

BUFFET STANDARD

Mark 1. These carriages are basically an open standard with two full window spaces removed to accommodate a buffet counter, and four seats removed to allow for a stock cupboard. All remaining vehicles now have fluorescent lighting. –/44 2T. Commonwealth bogies. ETS 3.

1861 has had its toilets replaced with store cupboards.

1813–32. Lot No. 30520 Wolverton 1960. 38 t.
1840. Lot No. 30507 Wolverton 1960. 37 t.
1859–63. Lot No. 30670 Wolverton 1961–62. 38 t.
1882. Lot No. 30702 Wolverton 1962. 38 t.

1813	x	**CH**	RV	*RV*	ZG	1860	x	**M**	WC	*WC*	CS
1832	x	**CH**	RV	*RV*	ZG	1861	x	**M**	WC	*WC*	CS
1840	v	**M**	WC	*WC*	CS	1863	x	**CH**	LS		CL
1859	x	**M**	SP	*SP*	BO	1882	x	**M**	WC	*WC*	CS

KITCHEN UNCLASSIFIED

Mark 1. These carriages were built as Unclassified Restaurants. They were rebuilt with buffet counters and 23 fixed polypropylene chairs, then further refurbished by fitting fluorescent lighting. Further modified for use as servery vehicle with seating removed and kitchen extended. ETS 2X.

1953. Lot No. 30575 Swindon 1960. B4/B5 bogies. 36.5 t.
1961. Lot No. 30632 Swindon 1961. Commonwealth bogies. 39 t.

| 1953 | | **VN** | WC | *WC* | CS | 1961 | x | **M** | WC | *WC* | CS |

HM THE QUEEN'S SALOON

Mark 3. Converted from an Open First built 1972. Consists of a lounge, bedroom and bathroom for HM The Queen, and a combined bedroom and bathroom for the Queen's dresser. One entrance vestibule has double doors. Air conditioned. BT10 bogies. ETS 9X.

Lot No. 30886 Wolverton 1977. 36 t.

| 2903 | (11001) | **RP** | NR | *RT* | | ZN |

HRH THE DUKE OF EDINBURGH'S SALOON

Mark 3. Converted from an Open Standard built 1972. Consists of a combined lounge/dining room, a bedroom and a shower room for the Duke, a kitchen and a valet's bedroom and bathroom. Air conditioned. BT10 bogies. ETS 15X.

Lot No. 30887 Wolverton 1977. 36 t.

| 2904 | (12001) | **RP** | NR | *RT* | | ZN |

ROYAL HOUSEHOLD SLEEPING CAR

Mark 3A. Built to similar specification as Sleeping Cars 10647–729. 12 sleeping compartments for use of Royal Household with a fixed lower berth and a hinged upper berth. 2T plus shower room. Air conditioned. BT10 bogies. ETS 11X.

Lot No. 31002 Derby/Wolverton 1985. 44 t.

| 2915 | | **RP** | NR | | *RT* | | ZN |

HRH THE PRINCE OF WALES'S DINING CAR

Mark 3. Converted from HST TRUK (kitchen car) built 1976. Large kitchen retained, but dining area modified for Royal use seating up to 14 at central table(s). Air conditioned. BT10 bogies. ETS 13X.

Lot No. 31059 Wolverton 1988. 43 t.

| 2916 | (40512) | **RP** | NR | | *RT* | | ZN |

ROYAL KITCHEN/HOUSEHOLD DINING CAR

Mark 3. Converted from HST TRUK built 1977. Large kitchen retained and dining area slightly modified with seating for 22 Royal Household members. Air conditioned. BT10 bogies. ETS 13X.

Lot No. 31084 Wolverton 1990. 43 t.

| 2917 | (40514) | **RP** | NR | | *RT* | | ZN |

ROYAL HOUSEHOLD CARS

Mark 3. Converted from HST TRUKs built 1976/77. Air conditioned. BT10 bogies. ETS 10X.

Lot Nos. 31083 (* 31085) Wolverton 1989. 41.05 t.

| 2918 | (40515) | **RP** | NR | | | | ZN |
| 2919 | (40518) * | **RP** | NR | | | | ZN |

ROYAL HOUSEHOLD COUCHETTES

Mark 2B. Converted from Corridor Brake First built 1969. Consists of luggage accommodation, guard's compartment, workshop area, 350 kW diesel generator and staff sleeping accommodation. B5 bogies. ETS 2X (when generator not in use). ETS index ?? (when generator in use).

Lot No. 31044 Wolverton 1986. 48 t.

| 2920 | (14109, 17109) | **RP** | NR | | *RT* | | ZN |

Mark 2B. Converted from Corridor Brake First built 1969. Consists of luggage accommodation, kitchen, brake control equipment and staff accommodation. B5 bogies. ETS 7X.

Lot No. 31086 Wolverton 1990. 41.5 t.

2921   (14107, 17107)   **RP**   NR   *RT*   ZN

HRH THE PRINCE OF WALES'S SLEEPING CAR

Mark 3B. Air conditioned. BT10 bogies. ETS 7X.

Lot No. 31035 Derby/Wolverton 1987.

2922   **RP**   NR   *RT*   ZN

ROYAL SALOON

Mark 3B. Air conditioned. BT10 bogies. ETS 6X.

Lot No. 31036 Derby/Wolverton 1987.

2923   **RP**   NR   *RT*   ZN

OPEN FIRST

Mark 1. 42/– 2T. ETS 3. Many now fitted with table lamps.

3058 was numbered DB 975313, 3068 was numbered DB 975606 and 3093 was numbered DB 977594 for a time when in departmental service for BR.

3045. Lot No. 30091 Doncaster 1954. B4 bogies. 33 t.
3058–68. Lot No. 30169 Doncaster 1955. B4 bogies. 33 t (* Commonwealth bogies 35 t).
3093. Lot No. 30472 BRCW 1959. B4 bogies. 33 t.
3096–3100. Lot No. 30576 BRCW 1959. B4 bogies. 33 t.

3045	x **CC**	LS	*LS*	CL		3096	x **M**	SP	*SP*	BO
3058	*x **M**	WC	*WC*	CS	FLORENCE	3097	**CH**	RV	*RV*	ZG
3066	**CC**	RV	*RV*	ZG		3098	x **CH**	RV	*RV*	ZG
3068	**CC**	RV	*RV*	ZG		3100	x **CC**	LS	*LS*	CL
3093	x **M**	WC	*WC*	CS	FLORENCE					

Later design with fluorescent lighting, aluminium window frames and Commonwealth bogies.

3128/36/41/43/46/47/48 were renumbered 1058/60/63/65/68/69/70 when reclassified Restaurant Open First, then 3600/05/08/09/06/04/10 when declassified to Open Standard, but have since regained their original numbers. 3136 was numbered DB 977970 for a time when in use with Serco Railtest as a Brake Force Runner.

3105 has had its luggage racks removed and has tungsten lighting.

3105–28. Lot No. 30697 Swindon 1962–63. 36 t.
3130–50. Lot No. 30717 Swindon 1963. 36 t.

3105	x	M	WC	*WC*	CS
3106	x	M	WC	*WC*	CS
3107	x	CC	LS		ZG
3110	x	CH	RV	*RV*	ZG
3112	x	CH	RV		ZG
3113	x	M	WC	*WC*	CS
3115	x	M	SP	*SP*	BO
3117	x	M	WC	*WC*	CS
3119	x	CH	RV	*RV*	ZG
3120		CH	RV	*RV*	ZG
3121		CH	RV	*RV*	ZG
3122	x	CC	LS	*LS*	CL
3123		CH	RV	*RV*	ZG

3125	x	CC	LS	*LS*	CL
3128	x	M	WC	*WC*	CS
3130	x	M	WC	*WC*	CS
3136	x	M	WC	*WC*	CS
3140	x	CC	LS		ZG
3141		CH	RV	*RV*	ZG
3143	x	M	WC	*WC*	CS
3146		CH	RV	*RV*	ZG
3147		CH	RV	*RV*	ZG
3148		CC	LS	*LS*	CL
3149		CH	RV	*RV*	ZG
3150		CC	SP	*SP*	BO

Names:

3105	JULIA		3128	VICTORIA
3106	ALEXANDRA		3130	PAMELA
3113	JESSICA		3136	DIANA
3117	CHRISTINA		3143	PATRICIA

OPEN FIRST

Mark 2D. Air conditioned. Stones equipment. 42/- 2T. B4 bogies. ETS 5.

Interior modified to Pullman Car standards with new seating, new panelling, tungsten lighting and table lights.

Lot No. 30821 Derby 1971–72. 34 t.

3174	†	VN	WC	*WC*	CS	GLAMIS
3182	†	VN	WC		CS	WARWICK
3188		PC	LS	*LS*	CL	CADAIR IDRIS

OPEN FIRST

Mark 2E. Air conditioned. Stones equipment. 42/- 2T (* 36/- 2T). B4 bogies. ETS 5.

Refurbished with new seats.
Interior modified to Pullman Car standards with new seating, new panelling, tungsten lighting and table lights.

Lot No. 30843 Derby 1972–73. 32.5 t. († 35.8 t).

3223		RV	LS		CL	DIAMOND
3229		PC	LS	*LS*	CL	SNOWDON
3231	*	PC	LS	*LS*	CL	BEN CRUACHAN
3232	dr	BG	WC		CS	
3240		RV	LS		CL	SAPPHIRE
3247	†	VN	WC	*WC*	CS	CHATSWORTH
3267	†	VN	WC	*WC*	CS	BELVOIR
3273	†	VN	WC	*WC*	CS	ALNWICK
3275	†	VN	WC	*WC*	CS	HARLECH

OPEN FIRST

Mark 2F. Air conditioned. 3278–3314/3359–79 have Stones equipment, other
have Temperature Ltd. All refurbished in the 1980s with power-operate
vestibule doors, new panels and new seat trim. 42/– 2T. B4 bogies. d. ETS 5×

r Further refurbished with table lamps and modified seats with burgundy
   seat trim.

3278–3314. Lot No. 30845 Derby 1973. 33.5 t.
3325–3426. Lot No. 30859 Derby 1973–74. 33.5 t.
3431–3438. Lot No. 30873 Derby 1974–75. 33.5 t.

3278	r	**BG**	RV	*RV*	BU		3356	r	**BG**	RV	*RV*	BU
3304	r	**BG**	RV	*RV*	BU		3359	r	**M**	WC	*WC*	CS
3312		**PC**	LS	*LS*	CL		3360	r	**PC**	WC	*WC*	CS
3313	r	**M**	WC	*WC*	CS		3362	r	**PC**	WC	*WC*	CS
3314	r	**BG**	RV	*RV*	BU		3364	r	**BG**	RV	*RV*	BU
3325	r	**V**	RV		ZG		3384	r	**PC**	LS	*LS*	CL
3326	r	**M**	WC	*WC*	CS		3386	r	**BG**	RV	*RV*	BU
3330	r	**CC**	LS	*LS*	CL		3390	r	**BG**	RV	*RV*	BU
3333	r	**BG**	RV	*RV*	BU		3392	r	**M**	WC	*WC*	CS
3340	r	**BG**	RV	*RV*	BU		3395	r	**M**	WC	*WC*	CS
3344	r	**PC**	LS	*LS*	CL		3397	r	**BG**	RV	*RV*	BU
3345	r	**BG**	RV	*RV*	BU		3426	r	**PC**	LS	*LS*	CL
3348	r	**PC**	LS	*LS*	CL		3431	r	**M**	WC	*WC*	CS
3350	r	**M**	WC	*WC*	CS		3438	r	**PC**	LS	*LS*	CL
3352	r	**M**	WC	*WC*	CS							

Names:

3312	HELVELLYN		3384	PEN-Y-GHENT
3344	SCAFELL		3426	BEN NEVIS
3348	INGLEBOROUGH		3438	BEN LOMOND

OPEN STANDARD

Mark 1. –/64 2T. ETS 4.

4831–36. Lot No. 30506 Wolverton 1959. Commonwealth bogies. 37 t.
4854/56. Lot No. 30525 Wolverton 1959–60. B4 bogies. 33 t.

4831	x	**M**	SP	*SP*	BO		4854	x	**M**	WC	*WC*	CS
4832	x	**M**	SP	*SP*	BO		4856	x	**M**	SP	*SP*	BO
4836	x	**M**	SP	*SP*	BO							

OPEN STANDARD

Mark 1. Commonwealth bogies. –/64 2T. ETS 4.

4905. Lot No. 30646 Wolverton 1961. 36 t.
4927–5044. Lot No. 30690 Wolverton 1961–62. 37 t.

4905	x	**M**	WC	*WC*	CS	4984	x	**M**	WC	*WC*	CS
4927	x	**CC**	RV	*RV*	ZG	4991		**CH**	RV	*RV*	ZG
4931	x	**M**	WC	*WC*	CS	4994	x	**M**	WC	*WC*	CS
4940	x	**M**	WC	*WC*	CS	4998		**CH**	RV	*RV*	ZG
4946	x	**CH**	RV	*RV*	ZG	5009	x	**CH**	RV	*RV*	ZG
4949	x	**CH**	RV	*RV*	ZG	5028	x	**M**	SP	*SP*	BO
4951	x	**M**	WC	*WC*	CS	5032	x	**M**	WC	*WC*	CS
4954	v	**M**	WC	*WC*	CS	5033	x	**M**	WC	*WC*	CS
4959		**CH**	RV	*RV*	ZG	5035	x	**M**	WC	*WC*	CS
4960	x	**M**	WC	*WC*	CS	5044	x	**M**	WC	*WC*	CS
4973	x	**M**	WC	*WC*	CS						

OPEN STANDARD

Mark 2. Pressure ventilated. –/64 2T. B4 bogies. ETS 4.

Lot No. 30751 Derby 1965–67. 32 t.

5157	v	**CH**	VT	*VT*	TM	5200	v	**M**	WC	*WC*	CS
5171	v	**M**	WC	*WC*	CS	5212	v	**CH**	VT	*VT*	TM
5177	v	**CH**	VT	*VT*	TM	5216	v	**M**	WC	*WC*	CS
5191	v	**CH**	VT	*VT*	TM	5222	v	**M**	WC	*WC*	CS
5198	v	**CH**	VT	*VT*	TM						

OPEN STANDARD

Mark 2. Pressure ventilated. –/48 2T. B4 bogies. ETS 4.

Lot No. 30752 Derby 1966. 32 t.

5229		**M**	WC	*WC*	CS	5239		**M**	WC	*WC*	CS
5236	v	**M**	WC	*WC*	CS	5249	v	**M**	WC	*WC*	CS
5237	v	**M**	WC	*WC*	CS						

OPEN STANDARD

Mark 2A. Pressure ventilated. –/64 2T (w –/62 2T). B4 bogies. ETS 4.

Facelifted vehicles.

5278–92. Lot No. 30776 Derby 1967–68. 32 t.
5366–5419. Lot No. 30787 Derby 1968. 32 t.

5278		**M**	WC	*WC*	CS	5366	f	**CC**	LS	*LS*	CL
5292	f	**CC**	RV		BU	5419	w	**M**	WC	*WC*	CS

OPEN STANDARD

Mark 2B. Pressure ventilated. –/62. B4 bogies. ETS 4.

Lot No. 30791 Derby 1969. 32 t.

| 5487 | | **M** | WC | *WC* | CS |

OPEN STANDARD

Mark 2E. Air conditioned. Stones equipment. Refurbished with new interior panelling. –/64 2T. B4 bogies. d. ETS 5.

s Modified design of seat headrest and centre luggage stack. –/60 2T.

5787. Lot No. 30837 Derby 1972. 33.5 t.
5810. Lot No. 30844 Derby 1972–73. 33.5 t.

| 5787 | s | **DS** | DR | *DR* | KM | | 5810 | | **DR** | LO | | CN |

OPEN STANDARD

Mark 2F. Air conditioned. Temperature Ltd equipment. InterCity 70 seats. All were refurbished in the 1980s with power-operated vestibule doors, new panels and seat trim. They have subsequently undergone a second refurbishment with carpets and new seat trim. –/64 2T. B4 bogies. d. ETS 5X.

q Fitted with two wheelchair spaces. –/60 2T 2W.
s Fitted with centre luggage stack. –/60 2T.
t Fitted with centre luggage stack and wheelchair space. –/58 2T 1W.
† Retention toilets.

5910–55. Lot No. 30846 Derby 1973. 33 t.
5961–6158. Lot No. 30860 Derby 1973–74. 33 t.
6173–83. Lot No. 30874 Derby 1974–75. 33 t.

5910	q	**V**	RV		BU		5991		**CC**	LS	*LS*	CL
5912		**PC**	LS	*LS*	CL		5995	†	**DS**	NR		CF
5919	† pt	**DR**	LO		CN		5998		**BG**	RV	*RV*	BU
5921		**AR**	RV	*RV*	BU		6000	t	**M**	WC	*WC*	CS
5929		**BG**	RV	*RV*	BU		6001	†	**DS**	NR		CF
5937		**DS**	DR	*DR*	KM		6006		**AR**	RV		BU
5945		**SR**	RV		BU		6008	† s	**DS**	NR		CF
5950		**AR**	RV	*RV*	BU		6012		**M**	WC	*WC*	CS
5952		**BG**	RV	*RV*	BU		6021		**PC**	WC	*WC*	CS
5955		**SR**	RV		BU		6022	s	**M**	WC	*WC*	CS
5961	pt	**BG**	RV	*RV*	BU		6024		**BG**	RV	*RV*	BU
5964		**AR**	RV	*RV*	BU		6027	q	**SR**	RV		BU
5965	t	**SR**	RV		BU		6042		**AR**	RV	*RV*	BU
5971	†	**DS**	NR		CF		6046	†	**DR**	LO		CN
5976	t	**SR**	RV		BU		6051		**BG**	RV	*RV*	BU
5985		**AR**	RV	*RV*	BU		6054		**BG**	RV	*RV*	BU
5987		**SR**	RV		BU		6064	†	**DS**	DR	*DR*	KM

6067	pt	**BG**	RV	*RV*	BU		6141	q	**V**	RV		BU
6103		**M**	WC	*WC*	CS		6158		**BG**	RV	*RV*	BU
6115	s	**M**	WC	*WC*	CS		6173	†	**DS**	DR	*DR*	KM
6117	†	**DS**	NR		CF		6176	t	**BG**	RV	*RV*	BU
6122	†	**DS**	NR		CF		6177	s	**SR**	RV		BU
6137	s pt	**SR**	RV		BU		6183	s	**SR**	RV		BU

BRAKE GENERATOR VAN

Mark 1. Renumbered 1989 from BR departmental series. Converted from Gangwayed Brake Van in 1973 to three-phase supply brake generator van for use with HST trailers. Modified 1999 for use with locomotive-hauled stock. B5 bogies. ETS index ??.

Lot No. 30400 Pressed Steel 1958.

6310	(81448, 975325)	**CH**	RV	*RV*		ZG

GENERATOR VAN

Mark 1. Converted from Gangwayed Brake Vans in 1992. B4 (* B5) bogies. ETS index 75.

6311. Lot No. 30162 Pressed Steel 1958. 37.25 t.
6312. Lot No. 30224 Cravens 1956. 37.25 t.
6313. Lot No. 30484 Pressed Steel 1958. 37.25 t.

6311	(80903, 92911)		**CC**	LS	*LS*	CL
6312	(81023, 92925)		**M**	WC	*WC*	CS
6313	(81553, 92167)	*	**PC**	BE	*BP*	SL

BUFFET STANDARD

Mark 2C. Converted from Open Standard by removal of one seating bay and replacing this with a counter with a space for a trolley, now replaced with a more substantial buffet. Adjacent toilet removed and converted to steward's washing area/store. Pressure ventilated. –/55 1T. B4 bogies. ETS 4.

Lot No. 30795 Derby 1969–70. 32.5 t.

6528	(5592)		**M**	WC	*WC*	CS

SLEEPER RECEPTION CAR

Mark 2F. Converted from Open First. These vehicles consist of pantry, microwave cooking facilities, seating area for passengers (with loose chairs, staff toilet plus two bars). Later refurbished again with new "sofa" seating as well as the loose chairs. Converted at RTC, Derby (6700), Ilford (6701–05) and Derby (6706–08). Air conditioned.

6700/01/03/05–08 have Stones equipment and 6702/04 have Temperature Ltd equipment. The number of seats per coach can vary but typically is 25/– 1T (12 seats as "sofa" seating and 13 loose chairs). B4 bogies. d. ETS 5X.

6705 and 6706 have been rebuilt as private saloons. Full details awaited.

6708 also carries the branding "THE HIPPOCRENE BAR".

6700–02/04/08. Lot No. 30859 Derby 1973–74. 33.5 t.
6703/05–07. Lot No. 30845 Derby 1973. 33.5 t.

6700	(3347)	**CA**	ER		YA	
6701	(3346)	**CA**	BR		ZM	
6702	(3421)	**FS**	ER		YA	
6703	(3308)	**CA**	ER		WO	
6704	(3341)	**FS**	ER		YA	
6705	(3310, 6430)	**CC**	LS	*LS*	CL	ARDNAMURCHAN
6706	(3283, 6421)	**CC**	LS	*LS*	CL	MOUNT MGAHINGA
6707	(3276, 6418)	**FS**	ER		YA	
6708	(3370)	**PC**	LS	*LS*	CL	MOUNT HELICON

BUFFET FIRST

Mark 2D. Converted from Buffet Standard by the removal of another seating bay and fitting a more substantial buffet counter with boiler and microwave oven. Now converted to First Class with new seating and end luggage stacks. Air conditioned. Stones equipment. 30/– 1T. B4 bogies. d. ETS 5. Lot No. 30822 Derby 1971. 33 t.

6723	(5641, 6662)	**M**	WC		CS
6724	(5721, 6665)	**M**	WC	*WC*	CS

OPEN BRAKE STANDARD WITH TROLLEY SPACE

Mark 2. This vehicle uses the same bodyshell as Mark 2 Corridor Brake Firsts and has First Class seat spacing and wider tables. Converted from Open Brake Standard by removal of one seating bay and replacing this with a counter with a space for a trolley. Adjacent toilet removed and converted to a steward's washing area/store. –/23. B4 bogies. ETS 4.

Lot No. 30757 Derby 1966. 31 t.

9101	(9398)	v	**CH**	VT	*VT*		TM

▲ Northern Belle-liveried Mark 1 Kitchen With Bar 1566 is seen at Great Strickland
n 19/09/20.   **Ian Beardsley**

BR chocolate & cream-liveried Mark 1 Kitchen Buffet Unclassified 1671 is seen
t Carlisle on 05/09/21.   **Ian Beardsley**

▲ BR carmine & cream-liveried Mark 1 Open First 3150 is seen near Sheffield on 16/09/21. **Robert Pritchard**

▼ BR maroon-liveried Mark 1 Open Standard 3860 is seen at Whitby on 02/07/21. This coach is passed for operation on the National Railway network on the Esk Valley Line only as part of the North Yorkshire Moors Railway fleet. **Ian Beardsley**

BR carmine & cream-liveried former Mark 2F Sleeper Reception Car 6705, now converted to a private saloon by Locomotive Services, is seen at Craigenhill on 05/03/21. **Robin Ralston**

▼ BR chocolate & cream-liveried Mark 2 Open Brake Standard 9101 is seen at Birmingham Moor Street on 29/07/21. **Ian Beardsley**

▲ WCRC maroon-liveried Mark 2 Open Brake Standard 9392 is seen at Garsdale on 03/08/21.
Robert Pritchard

▼ BR carmine & cream-liveried Sleeping Car With Pantry 10520 is seen at Craigenhill on 05/03/21.
Robin Ralston

▲ Repainted into BR InterCity Swallow livery, Mark 3B Open First 11075 (now operated by Locomotive Services) is seen at Crewe on 16/04/21. **Cliff Beeton**

▼ Virgin Trains East Coast-liveried Mark 4 Open First (Disabled) 11313, now operated by LNER, is seen at Shipley on 08/08/21. **Ian Beardsley**

▲ TransPennine Express-liveried Mark 5A Open First 11511 is seen at York on 07/07/21. **Robert Pritchard**

▼ In the erstwhile Greater Anglia livery, and now with DATS logos, Mark 3A Open Standard 12097 is seen at Leicester on 03/08/21. **Ian Beardsley**

▲ Chiltern Railways Mainline-liveried Mark 3A Open Standard 12623 is seen near Dorridge on 20/06/19. **Robert Pritchard**

▼ Caledonian Sleeper-liveried Mark 5 Sleeping Car 15319 is seen at Braidwood on 15/04/21. **Robin Ralston**

▲ BR Blue & Grey-liveried Mark 2B Couchette/Generator Coach 17105 is seen at Beighton Junction on 14/08/21.   **Ian Beardsley**

▼ BR chocolate & cream-liveried Mark 1 Kitchen Car 80042 is seen at Harwich International on 02/09/21.   **Ian Beardsley**

▲ WCRC maroon-liveried Mark 1 Open First 99122 (3106) is seen at Selside on the Settle–Carlisle line on 08/08/21. **Ian Beardsley**

▼ WCRC maroon-liveried Mark 1 Corridor Brake Standard 99723 (35459) is seen at Craigenhill on 12/03/21. **Robin Ralston**

▲ Carrying vinyls advertising the Royal National Lifeboat Institution, Transport for Wales Mark 4 Driving Brake Van 82229 is seen near Leominster with 5J7? 11.55 Crewe–Newport training run on 26/08/21. **Dave Gommersal**

▼ Midland Pullman-liveried HST Trailer Kitchen Buffet First 40801 is seen nea Carstairs on 15/08/21. **Robin Ralston**

▲ Rail Charter Services-liveried HST Trailer First 41187 is seen near Ribblehead on 03/08/21. **Robert Pritchard**

▼ CrossCountry-liveried HST Trailer Composite Kitchen 45004 is seen at Sheffield on 07/07/21. **Robert Pritchard**

▲ Great Western Railway-liveried HST Trailer Standard 48112 is seen at Cardiff Central on 20/09/21.   **Robert Pritchard**

▼ Royal Scotsman Service Car 99969 (Mark 3A Sleeping Car 10556) is seen at Perth on 15/04/19.   **Robert Pritchard**

Pullman Car Company-liveried Pullman Parlour First "ZENA" is seen at Worcester Shrub Hill on 03/07/21.   **Dave Gommersall**

Pullman Car Company-liveried Pullman Bar First 311 "EAGLE" is seen at Henley-in-Arden on 29/07/21.   **Ian Beardsley**

▲ Arlington Fleet Services-liveried EMU Translator Vehicle 64664 (converted from a Class 508 driving car) is seen near Saxilby on 18/09/20. **Robert Pritchard**

▼ Network Rail yellow-liveried Driving Trailer Coach 9714 is seen at Failford with 3Q62 11.10 Slateford–Ayr test train (powered by 37099) on 30/05/21. **Stuart Fowler**

▲ Network Rail Inspection Saloon 975025 (converted from a Class 202 DEMU RB) is seen at Henwick turnback siding in the company of 37421 on 25/05/21.
Dave Gommersall

▼ Network Rail yellow-liveried Overhead Line Equipment Test Coach 975091 is seen at Saxilby on 29/05/21.
Robert Pritchard

▲ Network Rail yellow-liveried New Measurement Train Test Coach 975814 is seen at Long Marston on 16/06/21. **Ian Beardsley**

▼ Network Rail yellow-liveried Ultrasonic Test Coach 999605 is seen at Doncaster on 07/07/21. **Ian Beardsley**

OPEN BRAKE STANDARD

Mark 2. These vehicles use the same bodyshell as Mark 2 Corridor Brake Firsts and have First Class seat spacing and wider tables. Pressure ventilated. –/31 1T. B4 bogies. ETS 4.

9104 was originally numbered 9401. It was renumbered when converted to Open Brake Standard with trolley space. Now returned to original layout.

Lot No. 30757 Derby 1966. 31.5 t.

9104	v	**M**	WC	*WC*	CS	9392	v	**M**	WC *WC*	CS
9391		**M**	WC	*WC*	CS					

OPEN BRAKE STANDARD

Mark 2D. Air conditioned. Stones Equipment. B4 bogies. d. pg. ETS 5.

r Refurbished with new interior panelling –/31 1T.
s Refurbished with new seating –/22 1TD.

Lot No. 30824 Derby 1971. 33 t.

9479	r	**PC**	LS	*LS*	CL	9493	s	**M**	WC *WC*	CS
9488	s	**SR**	DR	*DR*	KM					

OPEN BRAKE STANDARD

Mark 2E. Air conditioned. Stones Equipment. Refurbished with new interior panelling. –/32 1T (* –/30 1T 1W). B4 bogies. d. pg. ETS 5.

Non-standard livery: 9502 Pullman umber & cream.

s Modified design of seat headrest.

Lot No. 30838 Derby 1972. 33 t.

9497		**CA**	ER		WO	9507	s	**BG**	RV *RV*	BU
9502	s	**O**	BE	*BP*	SL	9509	s	**AV**	RV	BU
9504	s*	**BG**	RV	*RV*	BU					

OPEN BRAKE STANDARD

Mark 2F. Air conditioned. Temperature Ltd equipment. All were refurbished in the 1980s with power-operated vestibule doors, new panels and seat trim. All now further refurbished with carpets. –/32 1T (w –/30 1T 1W). B4 bogies. d. pg. ETS 5X.

9537 has had all its seats removed for the purpose of carrying luggage.

Lot No. 30861 Derby 1974. 34 t.

9513		**IC**	ER		WO	9526	n	**BG**	RV *RV*	BU
9520	nw	**AR**	RV	*RV*	BU	9527	n	**SR**	RV	BU
9521		**DS**	RV		BU	9537	n	**V**	RV	BU
9525		**DR**	LO		CN	9539		**SR**	RV	BU

DRIVING OPEN BRAKE STANDARD

Mark 2F. Air conditioned. Temperature Ltd equipment. Push & pull (tdm system). Converted from Open Brake Standard, these vehicles originally had half cabs at the brake end. They have since been refurbished and have had their cabs widened and the cab-end gangways removed. Five vehicles (9701–03/08/14) have been converted for use in Network Rail test trains and can be found in the Service Stock section of this book. –/30(+1) 1W B4 bogies. d. pg. Cowcatchers. ETS 5X.

Lot No. 30861 Derby 1974. Converted Glasgow 1979. Disc brakes. 34 t.

9704	(9512)	**DS**	DR		LW	9709	(9515)	**DS**	DR		LW
9705	(9519)	**DS**	DR		LW	9710	(9518)	**DS**	DR		BO
9707	(9511)	**DS**	DR		LW						

OPEN BRAKE UNCLASSIFIED

Mark 2E. Converted from Open Standard with new seating by Railcare, Wolverton. Air conditioned. Stones equipment. Five vehicles (9801/03/06/08/10) are currently used in Network Rail test trains and can be found in the Service Stock section of this book. –/31 2T. B4 bogies. d. ETS 4X.

9800/02. Lot No. 30837 Derby 1972. 33.5 t.
9804–09. Lot No. 30844 Derby 1972–73. 33.5 t.

9800	(5751)	**CA**	ER	WO	9805	(5833)	**FS**	ER	YA
9802	(5772)	**CA**	ER	YA	9807	(5851)	**FS**	ER	YA
9804	(5826)	**FS**	ER	CP	9809	(5890)	**FS**	ER	YA

KITCHEN BUFFET FIRST

Mark 3A. Air conditioned. Converted from HST catering vehicles and Mark Open Firsts. 18/– plus two seats for staff use (* 24/–, † 35/– 1T, t 23/– 1T 1W) BT10 bogies. d. ETS 14X.

† Refurbished Great Western Railway Sleeper coaches fitted with new Transcal seating.

Non-standard liveries:

10211 EWS dark maroon.
10241 Livery trials.

10211. Lot No. 30884 Derby 1977. 39.8 t.
10212–229. Lot No. 30878 Derby 1975–76. 39.8 t.
10237–259. Lot No. 30890 Derby 1979. 39.8 t.

10211	(40510)		**0**	DB	*DB*	TO	10229	(11059)	*	**GA**	ER		WO
10212	(11049)		**VT**	ER		YA	10237	(11022)	*	**B**	DA	*RO*	RJ
10217	(11051)	†	**GW**	P	*GW*	PZ	10241	(10009)	*	**0**	P		IL
10219	(11047)	†	**GW**	P	*GW*	PZ	10249	(10012)	t	**AW**	RO	*RO*	LR
10225	(11014)	†	**GW**	P	*GW*	PZ	10259	(10025)	t	**AW**	RO		CN

KITCHEN BUFFET FIRST

Mark 3A. Air conditioned. Rebuilt 2011–12 and fitted with sliding plug doors. Interiors originally refurbished for Wrexham & Shropshire with Primarius seating, a new kitchen area and universal-access toilet. Retention toilets. 0/– 1TD 1W. BT10 bogies. ETS 14X.

0271/273/274. Lot No. 30890 Derby 1979. 41.3 t.
0272. Lot No. 30884 Derby 1977. 41.3 t.

0271 (10018, 10236)	**CM**	AV	*CR*	AL
0272 (40517, 10208)	**CM**	AV	*CR*	AL
0273 (10021, 10230)	**CM**	AV	*CR*	AL
0274 (10010, 10255)	**CM**	AV	*CR*	AL

KITCHEN BUFFET STANDARD

Mark 4. Air conditioned. Rebuilt from First to Standard Class with bar adjacent to seating area instead of adjacent to end of coach. Retention toilets. –/30 1T. BT41 bogies. ETS 6X.

Lot No. 31045 Metro-Cammell 1989–92. 43.2 t.

0300	**VE**	E	*LN*	NL	10315	**VE**	E		ZB
0301	**GC**	TW		WS	10318	**GC**	TW		ZG
0305	**VE**	TW		ZB	10321	**GC**	TW		WS
0306	**VE**	E	*LN*	NL	10324	**VE**	E	*LN*	NL
0307	**VE**	E		WS	10325	**VE**	TW	*TW*	CF
0309	**VE**	E	*LN*	NL	10328	**VE**	TW	*TW*	CF
0311	**VE**	E	*LN*	NL	10330	**GC**	TW		WS
0312	**VE**	TW	*TW*	CF	10332	**VE**	E		WS
0313	**VE**	E	*LN*	NL	10333	**VE**	E	*LN*	NL

BUFFET STANDARD

Mark 3A. Air conditioned. Converted from Mark 3 Open Standard at Derby 2006. –/54. d. ETS 13X.

Lot No. 30877 Derby 1975–77. 37.8 t.

0406 (12020)	**GA**	EL	*RO*	LR

BUFFET STANDARD

Mark 3A. Air conditioned. Converted from Mark 3 Kitchen Buffet First 2015–16. –/54. BT10 bogies. d. ETS 13X.

0411. Lot No. 30884 Derby 1977. 37.8 t.
0413/416. Lot No. 30878 Derby 1975–76. 37.8 t.
0417. Lot No. 30890 Derby 1979. 37.8 t.

0411 (40519, 10200)	**IC**	LS	*LS*	CL
0413 (11034, 10214)	**GA**	ER		YA
0416 (11035, 10228)	**IC**	LS	*LS*	CL

SLEEPING CAR WITH PANTRY

Mark 3A. Air conditioned. Retention toilets. 12 compartments with a fixed lower berth and a hinged upper berth, plus an attendant's compartment (* 11 compartments with a fixed lower berth and a hinged upper berth + one compartment for a disabled person. 1TD). 2T. BT10 bogies. d. ETS 7X.

Non-standard livery: 10546 EWS dark maroon.

Lot No. 30960 Derby 1981–83. 41 t.

10501	**FS**	ER		YA	10584	**GW** P	*GW*	PZ
10502	**FS**	ER		YA	10589	**GW** P	*GW*	PZ
10504	**FS**	LS		KR	10590	**GW** P	*GW*	PZ
10513	**FS**	LS		KR	10594	**GW** P	*GW*	PZ
10519	**FS**	LS		CL	10596	**GW** P	*GW*	PZ
10520	**CC**	LS	*LS*	CL	10598	**FS** WC		CS
10532	**GW**	P	*GW*	PZ	10600	**FS** ER		YA
10534	**GW**	P	*GW*	PZ	10601 *	**GW** P	*GW*	PZ
10546	**O**	DB	*DB*	TO	10610	**FS** WC		CS
10551	**FS**	P		LA	10612 *	**GW** P	*GW*	PZ
10553	**FS**	P		LA	10614	**FS** WC		CS
10563	**GW**	P	*GW*	PZ	10616 *	**GW** P	*GW*	PZ

SLEEPING CAR

Mark 3A. Air conditioned. Retention toilets. 13 compartments with a fixed lower berth and a hinged upper berth (* 11 compartments with a fixed lower berth and a hinged upper berth + one compartment for a disabled person. 1TD). 2T. BT10 bogies. ETS 6X.

10734 was originally 2914 and used as a Royal Train staff sleeping car. It has 12 berths and a shower room and is ETS 11X.

10648–729. Lot No. 30961 Derby 1980–84. 43.5 t.
10734. Lot No. 31002 Derby/Wolverton 1985. 42.5 t.

10648 d*	**FS**	LS		KR	10703 d	**FS** WC		CS
10650 d*	**FS**	LS		KR	10714 d*	**FS** PO		CS
10675 d	**FS**	LS		KR	10718 d*	**FS** WC		CS
10683 d	**FS**	LS		KR	10719 d*	**FS** PO		CS
10688 d	**PC**	LS	*LS*	CL	10729	**VN** WC	*WC*	CS
10699 d*	**FS**	ER		YA	10734	**VN** WC	*WC*	CS

Names:

10729	CREWE	10734 BALMORAL

OPEN FIRST

Mark 3A. Air conditioned. All refurbished with table lamps and new seat cushions and trim. 48/– 2T. BT10 bogies. d. ETS 6X.

Non-standard livery: 11039 EWS dark maroon.

Lot No. 30878 Derby 1975–76. 34.3 t.

11018	**VT**	DA	*RO*	RJ		11048	**VT**	DA	*RO*	RJ
11039	**O**	DB	*DB*	TO					

OPEN FIRST

Mark 3B. Air conditioned. InterCity 80 seats. All refurbished with table lamps and new seat cushions and trim. Retention toilets. 48/– 1T. BT10 bogies. d. ETS 6X.

†   Fitted with disabled toilet and reduced seating, including three Compin Pegasus seats. 37/– 1TD 2W.

Non-standard livery: 11074 Original HST prototype grey & BR blue.

Lot No. 30982 Derby 1985. 36.5 t.

11068	**IC**	LS	*LS*	CL		11090 †	**GA**	DA	*RO*	RJ
11070	**IC**	LS	*LS*	CL		11091	**IC**	LS	*LS*	CL
11074	**O**	DA	*RO*	RJ		11092 †	**GA**	EL	*RO*	LR
11075	**IC**	LS	*LS*	CL		11093 †	**GA**	EL	*RO*	LR
11076	**IC**	LS	*LS*	CL		11095 †	**GA**	PO		YA
11077	**IC**	LS	*LS*	CL		11098 †	**IC**	LS	*LS*	CL
11078 †	**GA**	ER		YA		11099 †	**GA**	EL	*RO*	LR
11087 †	**IC**	LS	*LS*	CL		11101 †	**GA**	EL	*RO*	LR
11088 †	**GA**	P		BU					

OPEN FIRST

Mark 4. Air conditioned. Rebuilt with new interior by Bombardier Wakefield 2003–05 (some converted from Standard Class vehicles). Retention toilets. 51/– 1T (plus 2 seats for staff use). BT41 bogies. ETS 6X.

11229. Lot No. 31046 Metro-Cammell 1989–92. 41.3 t.
11279–11295. Lot No. 31049 Metro-Cammell 1989–92. 41.3 t.

11229		**VE**	E	*LN*	NL		11286 (12482)	**VE**	E	*LN*	NL
11279 (12521)	**VE**	E	*LN*	NL		11288 (12517)	**VE**	E	*LN*	NL
11284 (12487)	**VE**	E	*LN*	NL		11295 (12475)	**VE**	E	*LN*	NL
11285 (12537)	**VE**	E	*LN*	NL					

OPEN FIRST (DISABLED)

Mark 4. Air conditioned. Rebuilt from Open First by Bombardier Wakefield 2003–05. Retention toilets. 42/– 1TD 1W. BT41 bogies. ETS 6X.

Lot No. 31046 Metro-Cammell 1989–92. 40.7 t.

11306 (11276) **VE**	E	*LN*	NL	11318 (11251) **VE**	E		ZB
11308 (11263) **VE**	E	*LN*	NL	11319 (11247) **GC**	TW		ZG
11309 (11259) **VE**	E		WS	11320 (11255) **GC**	TW		WS
11312 (11225) **VE**	E	*LN*	NL	11321 (11245) **GC**	TW		WS
11313 (11210) **VE**	E	*LN*	NL	11322 (11228) **GC**	TW		WS
11314 (11207) **VE**	E		WS	11323 (11235) **VE**	TW	*TW*	CF
11315 (11238) **VE**	E	*LN*	NL	11324 (11253) **VE**	TW	*TW*	CF
11316 (11227) **VE**	E		WS	11325 (11231) **VE**	TW	*TW*	CF
11317 (11223) **VE**	E	*LN*	NL	11326 (11206) **VE**	E	*LN*	NL

OPEN FIRST

Mark 4. Air conditioned. Rebuilt from Open First by Bombardier Wakefield 2003–05. Separate area for 7 smokers, although smoking is no longer allowed. Retention toilets. 46/– 1TD 1W. BT41 bogies. ETS 6X.

Lot No. 31046 Metro-Cammell 1989–92. 42.1 t.

11404 (11202) **VE**	E		WS	11414 (11246) **VE**	E		WS
11406 (11205) **VE**	E	*LN*	NL	11415 (11208) **VE**	E	*LN*	NL
11408 (11218) **VE**	E	*LN*	NL	11416 (11254) **VE**	E		ZB
11409 (11262) **VE**	E		WS	11417 (11226) **VE**	E	*LN*	NL
11412 (11209) **VE**	E	*LN*	NL	11418 (11222) **VE**	E		ZB
11413 (11212) **VE**	E	*LN*	NL	11426 (11252) **VE**	E	*LN*	NL

OPEN FIRST

CAF Mark 5A. Air conditioned. New TransPennine Express coaches. Retention toilets. 30/– 1TD 2W. CAF bogies. ETS XX.

CAF Beasain 2017–18. 32.7 t.

11501	**TP**	BN	*TP*	MA	11508	**TP**	BN	*TP*	MA
11502	**TP**	BN	*TP*	MA	11509	**TP**	BN	*TP*	MA
11503	**TP**	BN	*TP*	MA	11510	**TP**	BN	*TP*	MA
11504	**TP**	BN	*TP*	MA	11511	**TP**	BN	*TP*	MA
11505	**TP**	BN	*TP*	MA	11512	**TP**	BN	*TP*	MA
11506	**TP**	BN	*TP*	MA	11513	**TP**	BN	*TP*	MA
11507	**TP**	BN	*TP*	MA					

OPEN STANDARD

Mark 3A. Air conditioned. All refurbished with modified seat backs and new layout and further refurbished with new seat trim. –/76 2T († –/70 2T 1W, t –/72 2T, z –/70 1TD 1T 2W). BT10 bogies. d. ETS 6X.

* Further refurbished with more unidirectional seating and one toilet removed. Retention toilets. –/80 1T.
s Refurbished Sleeper day coaches fitted with new Transcal seating to a 2+2 layout and a universal access toilet. Retention toilets. –/65 1TD 1W.

12171 was converted from Open Composite 11910, formerly Open First 11010.

Non-standard livery: 12092 Original HST prototype grey & BR blue.

12017–167. Lot No. 30877 Derby 1975–77. 34.3 t.
12171. Lot No. 30878 Derby 1975–76. 34.3 t.

12017	t	**CM**	ER		YA	12100	s	**GW**	P	*GW*	PZ
12021	*	**GA**	ER		YA	12111	*	**GA**	LS		CL
12032	*	**GA**	DA	*RO*	RJ	12122	z	**VT**	DA	*RO*	RJ
12036	†	**CM**	ER		YA	12125		**GA**	EL	*RO*	LR
12043	†	**CM**	ER		YA	12133		**VT**	DA	*RO*	RJ
12061		**GA**	PM		LM	12137	*	**GA**	PM		LM
12064	*	**GA**	DA	*RO*	RJ	12138		**VT**	DA	*RO*	RJ
12078		**VT**	DA	*RO*	RJ	12142	s	**GW**	P	*GW*	PZ
12079	*	**GA**	PM		LM	12146	*	**GA**	PM		LM
12090	*	**GA**	PM		LM	12154	*	**GA**	EL	*RO*	LR
12091	*	**GA**	DA	*RO*	RJ	12161	s	**GW**	P	*GW*	PZ
12092		**O**	DA	*RO*	RJ	12164	*	**GA**	PM		LM
12094		**CM**	ER		YA	12167	*	**GA**	PM		LM
12097	*	**GA**	DA	*RO*	RJ	12171	*	**IC**	LS	*LS*	CL
12098	*	**GA**	ER		YA						

OPEN STANDARD

Mark 3A (†) or Mark 3B. Air conditioned. Converted from Mark 3A or 3B Open First. Fitted with Grammer seating. –/70 2T 1W. BT10 bogies. d. ETS 6X.

12176–181/185. Mark 3B. Lot No. 30982 Derby 1985. 38.5 t.
12182–184. Mark 3A. Lot No. 30878 Derby 1975–76. 38.5 t.

12176	(11064)		**AW**	RO	*RO*	LR
12177	(11065)		**AW**	RO		BR
12178	(11071)		**AW**	RO		BR
12179	(11083)		**AW**	RO		BR
12180	(11084)		**AW**	RO	*RO*	LR
12181	(11086)		**AW**	RO		BR
12182	(11013)	†	**AW**	RO		ZA
12183	(11027)	†	**AW**	RO		BR
12184	(11044)	†	**AW**	RO		BR
12185	(11089)		**AW**	RO		BR

OPEN STANDARD (END)

Mark 4. Air conditioned. Rebuilt with new interior by Bombardier Wakefield 2003–05. Separate area for 26 smokers, although smoking is no longer allowed. Retention toilets. –/76 1T. BT41 bogies. ETS 6X.

12202–231. Lot No. 31047 Metro-Cammell 1989–91. 39.5 t.

12202	**VE**	E		ZB		12219	**VE**	TW	*TW*	CF
12203	**VE**	E		WS		12220	**VE**	E	*LN*	NL
12205	**VE**	E	*LN*	NL		12222	**GC**	TW		WS
12208	**VE**	E	*LN*	NL		12223	**VE**	E	*LN*	NL
12209	**VE**	E		WS		12224	**GC**	TW		WS
12210	**GC**	TW		WS		12225	**VE**	TW	*TW*	CF
12211	**GC**	TW		ZG		12226	**VE**	E	*LN*	NL
12212	**VE**	E	*LN*	NL		12228	**VE**	E	*LN*	NL
12213	**VE**	E		ZB		12229	**VE**	E		WS
12214	**VE**	E	*LN*	NL		12230	**VE**	E		WS
12215	**VE**	TW		ZB		12231	**VE**	E		WS
12217	**VE**	TW	*TW*	CF						

OPEN STANDARD (DISABLED)

Mark 4. Air conditioned. Rebuilt with new interior by Bombardier Wakefield 2003–05. Retention toilets. –/68 2W 1TD. BT41 bogies. ETS 6X.

12300–330. Lot No. 31048 Metro-Cammell 1989–91. 39.4 t.

12300	**VE**	E		WS		12313	**VE**	E	*LN*	NL
12303	**VE**	E	*LN*	NL		12315	**VE**	TW		ZB
12304	**VE**	TW		ZB		12316	**GC**	TW		WS
12305	**VE**	E		WS		12323	**GC**	TW		WS
12308	**VE**	E		WS		12324	**VE**	TW		ZB
12309	**VE**	E	*LN*	NL		12325	**VE**	E	*LN*	NL
12310	**GC**	TW		ZG		12326	**GC**	TW		WS
12311	**VE**	E	*LN*	NL		12328	**VE**	E	*LN*	NL
12312	**VE**	E		ZB		12330	**VE**	E	*LN*	NL

OPEN STANDARD

Mark 4. Air conditioned. Rebuilt with new interior by Bombardier Wakefield 2003–05. Retention toilets. –/76 1T. BT41 bogies. ETS 6X.

12405 is the second coach to carry that number. It was built from the bodyshell originally intended for 12221. The original 12405 became 12232.

Lot No. 31049 Metro-Cammell 1989–92. 40.8 t.

12404	**VE**	E	*LN*	NL		12415	**VE**	E		WS
12405	**VE**	E		WS		12417	**VE**	E		WS
12406	**VE**	E	*LN*	NL		12419	**VE**	E		WS
12407	**VE**	E	*LN*	NL		12420	**VE**	E	*LN*	NL
12409	**VE**	E	*LN*	NL		12421	**VE**	E		WS
12410	**VE**	E		WS		12422	**VE**	E	*LN*	NL

12423	**VE**	E		WS	12454	**VE**	TW	*TW*	CF
12424	**VE**	E	*LN*	NL	12461	**GC**	TW		WS
12426	**VE**	E	*LN*	NL	12465	**VE**	E	*LN*	NL
12427	**VE**	E	*LN*	NL	12467	**VE**	E		ZB
12428	**VE**	E		ZB	12468	**VE**	E		WS
12429	**VE**	E	*LN*	NL	12469	**VE**	E	*LN*	NL
12430	**VE**	E	*LN*	NL	12474	**VE**	E	*LN*	NL
12431	**VE**	E	*LN*	NL	12477	**GC**	TW		WS
12432	**VE**	E	*LN*	NL	12480	**VE**	E		WS
12433	**VE**	E		ZB	12481	**VE**	E	*LN*	NL
12434	**GC**	TW		ZG	12483	**VE**	E		WS
12436	**VE**	E		WS	12484	**VE**	E		WS
12437	**VE**	E		WS	12485	**VE**	E	*LN*	NL
12442	**VE**	E	*LN*	NL	12486	**VE**	E		WS
12443	**VE**	E		WS	12513	**VE**	E		WS
12444	**VE**	E	*LN*	NL	12514	**VE**	E		WS
12446	**VE**	TW	*TW*	CF	12515	**VE**	E	*LN*	NL
12447	**VE**	TW	*TW*	CF	12518	**VE**	E		WS
12452	**GC**	TW		WS	12520	**VE**	E		WS
12453	**VE**	E		WS	12526	**VE**	E		WS

OPEN STANDARD

Mark 3A. Air conditioned. Rebuilt 2011–13 and fitted with sliding plug doors. Original InterCity 70 seating retained but mainly arranged around tables. Retention toilets. –/72(+6) or * –/69(+4) 1T. BT10 bogies. ETS 6X.

12602–609/614–616/618/620. Lot No. 30877 Derby 1975–77. 36.2 t (* 37.1 t)
12601/613/617–619/621/623/625/627. Lot No. 30878 Derby 1975–76. 36.2 t (* 37.1 t).

12602	(12072)		**CM**	AV	*CR*	AL
12603	(12053)	*	**CM**	AV	*CR*	AL
12604	(12131)		**CM**	AV	*CR*	AL
12605	(11040)	*	**CM**	AV	*CR*	AL
12606	(12048)		**CM**	AV	*CR*	AL
12607	(12038)	*	**CM**	AV	*CR*	AL
12608	(12069)		**CM**	AV	*CR*	AL
12609	(12014)	*	**CM**	AV	*CR*	AL
12610	(12117)		**CM**	AV	*CR*	AL
12613	(11042, 12173)		**CM**	AV	*CR*	AL
12614	(12145)		**CM**	AV	*CR*	AL
12615	(12059)	*	**CM**	AV	*CR*	AL
12616	(12127)		**CM**	AV	*CR*	AL
12617	(11052, 12174)	*	**CM**	AV	*CR*	AL
12618	(11008, 12169)		**CM**	AV	*CR*	AL
12619	(11058, 12175)		**CM**	AV	*CR*	AL
12620	(12124)		**CM**	AV	*CR*	AL
12621	(11046)	*	**CM**	AV	*CR*	AL
12623	(11019)		**CM**	AV	*CR*	AL
12625	(11030)	*	**CM**	AV	*CR*	AL
12627	(11054)	*	**CM**	AV	*CR*	AL

OPEN STANDARD

CAF Mark 5A. Air conditioned. New TransPennine Express coaches. Retention toilets. –/69 1T (* –/59(+6) 1T + bike spaces). CAF bogies. ETS XX.

CAF Beasain 2017–18. 31.8 t (* 31.6 t).

12701	**TP**	BN	*TP*	MA	12721 *	**TP**	BN	*TP*	MA
12702	**TP**	BN	*TP*	MA	12722	**TP**	BN	*TP*	MA
12703 *	**TP**	BN	*TP*	MA	12723	**TP**	BN	*TP*	MA
12704	**TP**	BN	*TP*	MA	12724 *	**TP**	BN	*TP*	MA
12705	**TP**	BN	*TP*	MA	12725	**TP**	BN	*TP*	MA
12706 *	**TP**	BN	*TP*	MA	12726	**TP**	BN	*TP*	MA
12707	**TP**	BN	*TP*	MA	12727 *	**TP**	BN	*TP*	MA
12708	**TP**	BN	*TP*	MA	12728	**TP**	BN	*TP*	MA
12709 *	**TP**	BN	*TP*	MA	12729	**TP**	BN	*TP*	MA
12710	**TP**	BN	*TP*	MA	12730 *	**TP**	BN	*TP*	MA
12711	**TP**	BN	*TP*	MA	12731	**TP**	BN	*TP*	MA
12712 *	**TP**	BN	*TP*	MA	12732	**TP**	BN	*TP*	MA
12713	**TP**	BN	*TP*	MA	12733 *	**TP**	BN	*TP*	MA
12714	**TP**	BN	*TP*	MA	12734	**TP**	BN	*TP*	MA
12715 *	**TP**	BN	*TP*	MA	12735	**TP**	BN	*TP*	MA
12716	**TP**	BN	*TP*	MA	12736 *	**TP**	BN	*TP*	MA
12717	**TP**	BN	*TP*	MA	12737	**TP**	BN	*TP*	MA
12718 *	**TP**	BN	*TP*	MA	12738	**TP**	BN	*TP*	MA
12719	**TP**	BN	*TP*	MA	12739 *	**TP**	BN	*TP*	MA
12720	**TP**	BN	*TP*	MA					

DRIVING OPEN BRAKE STANDARD

CAF Mark 5A. Air conditioned. New TransPennine Express coaches. –/64. CAF bogies. ETS XX.

CAF Irun 2017–18. 32.9 t.

12801	**TP**	BN	*TP*	MA	12808	**TP**	BN	*TP*	MA
12802	**TP**	BN	*TP*	MA	12809	**TP**	BN	*TP*	MA
12803	**TP**	BN	*TP*	MA	12810	**TP**	BN	*TP*	MA
12804	**TP**	BN	*TP*	MA	12811	**TP**	BN	*TP*	MA
12805	**TP**	BN	*TP*	MA	12812	**TP**	BN	*TP*	MA
12806	**TP**	BN	*TP*	MA	12813	**TP**	BN	*TP*	MA
12807	**TP**	BN	*TP*	MA	12814	**TP**	BN	*TP*	MA

CORRIDOR FIRST

Mark 1. Seven compartments. 42/– 2T. B4 bogies. ETS 3.
Lot No. 30381 Swindon 1959. 33 t.
Lot No. 30667 Swindon 1962. Commonwealth bogies. 36 t.

13227 x	**CC**	LS	*LS*	CL	13230 xk	**M**	SP	*SP*	BO	
13229 xk	**M**	SP	*SP*	BO	13306 x	**M**	WC	*WC*	CS	

Name: 13306   JOANNA

OPEN FIRST

Mark 1 converted from Corridor First in 2013–14. 42/– 2T. Commonwealth bogies. ETS 3.

Lot No. 30667 Swindon 1962. 35 t.

13320 x   **M** WC *WC*   CS   ANNA

CORRIDOR FIRST

Mark 2A. Seven compartments. Pressure ventilated. 42/– 2T. B4 bogies ETS 4.

Lot No. 30774 Derby 1968. 33 t.

13440 v   **M** WC *WC*   CS

SLEEPER SEATED CARRIAGE WITH BRAKE

CAF Mark 5. Air conditioned. Retention toilets. –/31 1TD 1W. CAF bogies ETS XX.

CAF Irun 2016–18. 32.5 t.

15001	**CA**	LF	*CA*	PO	15007	**CA**	LF	*CA*	PO
15002	**CA**	LF	*CA*	PO	15008	**CA**	LF	*CA*	PO
15003	**CA**	LF	*CA*	PO	15009	**CA**	LF	*CA*	PO
15004	**CA**	LF	*CA*	PO	15010	**CA**	LF	*CA*	PO
15005	**CA**	LF	*CA*	PO	15011	**CA**	LF	*CA*	PO
15006	**CA**	LF	*CA*	PO				

SLEEPER LOUNGE CAR

CAF Mark 5. Air conditioned. –/30 or –/28 1W. CAF bogies. ETS XX.

CAF Beasain 2016–18. 35.5 t.

15101	**CA**	LF	*CA*	PO	15106	**CA**	LF	*CA*	PO
15102	**CA**	LF	*CA*	PO	15107	**CA**	LF	*CA*	PO
15103	**CA**	LF	*CA*	PO	15108	**CA**	LF	*CA*	PO
15104	**CA**	LF	*CA*	PO	15109	**CA**	LF	*CA*	PO
15105	**CA**	LF	*CA*	PO	15110	**CA**	LF	*CA*	PO

SLEEPING CAR (FULLY ACCESSIBLE)

CAF Mark 5. Air conditioned. Two fully accessible berths
one with double bed, one with foldable upper bed), two berths with double
beds and en-suite toilets and showers, two berths with foldable upper
beds. 2TD 2T, plus two showers. CAF bogies. ETS XX.

CAF Castejon/Irun 2016–18. 35.5 t.

15201	**CA**	LF	*CA*	PO	15208	**CA**	LF	*CA*	PO
15202	**CA**	LF	*CA*	PO	15209	**CA**	LF	*CA*	PO
15203	**CA**	LF	*CA*	PO	15210	**CA**	LF	*CA*	PO
15204	**CA**	LF	*CA*	PO	15211	**CA**	LF	*CA*	PO
15205	**CA**	LF	*CA*	PO	15212	**CA**	LF	*CA*	PO
15206	**CA**	LF	*CA*	PO	15213	**CA**	LF	*CA*	PO
15207	**CA**	LF	*CA*	PO	15214	**CA**	LF	*CA*	PO

SLEEPING CAR

CAF Mark 5. Air conditioned. Retention toilets. 6 en-suite toilet/shower and
4 non en-suite compartments with a fixed lower berth and hinged upper
berth. 7T. CAF bogies. ETS XX.

CAF Beasain 2016–18. 38.0 t.

15301	**CA**	LF	*CA*	PO	15321	**CA**	LF	*CA*	PO
15302	**CA**	LF	*CA*	PO	15322	**CA**	LF	*CA*	PO
15303	**CA**	LF	*CA*	PO	15323	**CA**	LF	*CA*	PO
15304	**CA**	LF	*CA*	PO	15324	**CA**	LF	*CA*	PO
15305	**CA**	LF	*CA*	PO	15325	**CA**	LF	*CA*	PO
15306	**CA**	LF	*CA*	PO	15326	**CA**	LF	*CA*	PO
15307	**CA**	LF	*CA*	PO	15327	**CA**	LF	*CA*	PO
15308	**CA**	LF	*CA*	PO	15328	**CA**	LF	*CA*	PO
15309	**CA**	LF	*CA*	PO	15329	**CA**	LF	*CA*	PO
15310	**CA**	LF	*CA*	PO	15330	**CA**	LF	*CA*	PO
15311	**CA**	LF	*CA*	PO	15331	**CA**	LF	*CA*	PO
15312	**CA**	LF	*CA*	PO	15332	**CA**	LF	*CA*	PO
15313	**CA**	LF	*CA*	PO	15333	**CA**	LF	*CA*	PO
15314	**CA**	LF	*CA*	PO	15334	**CA**	LF	*CA*	PO
15315	**CA**	LF	*CA*	PO	15335	**CA**	LF	*CA*	PO
15316	**CA**	LF	*CA*	PO	15336	**CA**	LF	*CA*	PO
15317	**CA**	LF	*CA*	PO	15337	**CA**	LF	*CA*	PO
15318	**CA**	LF	*CA*	PO	15338	**CA**	LF	*CA*	PO
15319	**CA**	LF	*CA*	PO	15339	**CA**	LF	*CA*	PO
15320	**CA**	LF	*CA*	PO	15340	**CA**	LF	*CA*	PO

CORRIDOR BRAKE FIRST

Mark 1. Four compartments. 24/– 1T. Commonwealth bogies. ETS 2.

Lot No. 30668 Swindon 1961. 36 t.

17013	(14013)		**CC**	LS	ZG	
17018	(14018)	v	**CH**	VT	TM	BOTAURUS

CORRIDOR BRAKE FIRST

Mark 2A. Four compartments. Pressure ventilated. 24/– 1T. B4 bogies. ETS 4

17080/090 were numbered 35516/503 for a time when declassified.

17056. Lot No. 30775 Derby 1967–68. 32 t.
17080–102. Lot No. 30786 Derby 1968. 32 t.

17056 (14056)		**PC**	LS	*LS*	**CL**
17080 (14080)		**PC**	LS		**ZG**
17090 (14090)	v	**CH**	VT		**TM**
17102 (14102)		**M**	WC	*WC*	**CS**

COUCHETTE/GENERATOR COACH

Mark 2B. Formerly part of Royal Train. Converted from Corridor Brake First built 1969. Consists of luggage accommodation, guard's compartment, 350 kW diesel generator and staff sleeping accommodation. Pressure ventilated. B5 bogies. ETS 5X (when generator not in use). ETS index ? (when generator in use).

Lot No. 30888 Wolverton 1977. 46 t.

17105 (14105, 2905)	**BG**	RV	*RV*	BU

CORRIDOR BRAKE FIRST

Mark 2D. Four compartments. Air conditioned. Stones equipment. 24/– 1T B4 Bogies. ETS 5.

Lot No. 30823 Derby 1971–72. 33.5 t.

17159 (14159)	d	**CC**	LS	*LS*	**CL**	
17167 (14167)		**VN**	WC	*WC*	**CS**	MOW COP

OPEN BRAKE UNCLASSIFIED

Mark 3B. Air conditioned. Fitted with hydraulic handbrake. Used as Sleeper day coaches. Refurbished with new Transcal seating 2018. 55/– 1T. BT1 bogies. pg. d. ETS 6X.

Lot No. 30990 Derby 1986. 35.8 t.

17173	**GW**	P	*GW*	PZ		17175	**GW** P	*GW*	PZ
17174	**GW**	P	*GW*	PZ					

CORRIDOR STANDARD

Mark 1. –/48 2T. Eight Compartments. Commonwealth bogies. ETS 4.
Currently in use as part of the Harry Potter World exhibition at Leavesden, near Watford.

Lot No. 30685 Derby 1961–62. 36 t.

18756 (25756)	x		**M**	WC		SH

CORRIDOR BRAKE COMPOSITE

Mark 1. There are two variants depending upon whether the Standard Class compartments have armrests. Each vehicle has two First Class and three Standard Class compartments. 12/18 2T (* 12/24 2T). Commonwealth bogies. ETS 2.

21241–245. Lot No. 30669 Swindon 1961–62. 36 t.
21256. Lot No. 30731 Derby 1963. 37 t.
21266–272. Lot No. 30732 Derby 1964. 37 t.

21241	x	**M**	SP	*SP*	BO		21266	x*	**M**	WC	*WC*	CS
21245	x	**M**	RV		ZG		21269	*	**CC**	RV	*RV*	ZG
21256	x	**M**	WC	*WC*	CS		21272	x*	**CH**	RV	*RV*	ZG

CORRIDOR BRAKE STANDARD

Mark 1. Four compartments. –/24 1T. ETS 2.

35185. Lot No. 30427 Wolverton 1959. B4 bogies. 33 t.
35459/465. Lot No. 30721 Wolverton 1963. Commonwealth bogies. 37 t.

35185	x	**M**	SP	*SP*	BO
35459	x	**M**	WC	*WC*	CS
35465	x	**CC**	LS	*LS*	CL

CORRIDOR BRAKE GENERATOR STANDARD

Mark 1. Four compartments. –/24 1T. Fitted with an ETS generator in the former luggage compartment. ETS 2 (when generator not in use). ETS index ?? (when generator in use).

Lot No. 30721 Wolverton 1963. Commonwealth bogies. 37 t.

35469	x	**CH**	RV	*RV*	ZG

BRAKE/POWER KITCHEN

Mark 2C. Pressure ventilated. Converted from Corridor Brake Firs
(declassified to Corridor Brake Standard) built 1970. Converted by Wes
Coast Railway Company 2000–01. Consists of 60 kVA generator, guard'
compartment and electric kitchen. B5 bogies. ETS ? (when generator not i
use). ETS index ?? (when generator in use).

Non-standard livery: Brown.

Lot No. 30796 Derby 1969–70. 32.5 t.

35511 (14130, 17130)	**0**	LS		CL

KITCHEN CAR

Mark 1. Converted 1989/2006/2017–19 from Kitchen Buffet Unclassified
80041/020 had buffet and seating area replaced with additional kitchen and
food preparation area. 80043 had a full length kitchen fitted. Fluorescen
lighting. Commonwealth or (†) B5 bogies. ETS 2X.

Lot No. 30628 Pressed Steel 1960–61. 39 t (* 36.4 t).

80041 (1690)	x	**M**	RV		ZG
80042 (1646)		**CH**	RV	RV	ZG
80043 (1680)	*	**PC**	LS	LS	CL
80044 (1659)	†	**CC**	LS	LS	CL

DRIVING BRAKE VAN (110 mph)

Mark 3B. Air conditioned. T4 bogies. dg. ETS 5X. Driving Brake Van
converted for use by Network Rail can be found in the Service Stock sectio
of this book.

Non-standard livery: 82146 All over silver with DB logos.

Lot No. 31042 Derby 1988. 45.2 t.

82107	**GA**	EL		BR	82138	**B**	DA	RO	RJ
82115	**B**	DA	RO	RJ	82139	**IC**	LS	LS	CL
82127	**IC**	LS	LS	CL	82146	**0**	DB	DB	TO
82136	**GA**	DA	RO	RJ					

DRIVING BRAKE VAN (140 mph)

Mark 4. Air conditioned. Swiss-built (SIG) bogies. dg. ETS 6X.

Advertising liveries:

82205 Flying Scotsman (red, white & purple).
82226 Alzheimer's Society Cymru (blue).
82229 Royal National Lifeboat Institution (black).

Lot No. 31043 Metro-Cammell 1988. 43.5 t.

2200	**GC**	TW		WS	82215	**VE**	E		ZB
2201	**GC**	TW		ZG	82216	**TW**	TW	*TW*	CF
2204	**VE**	E		WS	82218	**VE**	E		WS
2205	**AL**	E	*LN*	NL	82220	**VE**	TW		ZB
2206	**VE**	E		WS	82222	**VE**	E		ZB
2208	**VE**	E	*LN*	NL	82223	**VE**	E	*LN*	NL
2209	**VE**	E		WS	82225	**VE**	E	*LN*	NL
2210	**VE**	E		WS	82226	**AL**	TW	*TW*	CF
2211	**VE**	E	*LN*	NL	82227	**GC**	TW		WS
2212	**VE**	E	*LN*	NL	82229	**AL**	TW	*TW*	CF
2213	**VE**	E	*LN*	NL	82230	**GC**	TW		WS
2214	**VE**	E	*LN*	NL					

DRIVING BRAKE VAN (100 mph)

Mark 3B. Air conditioned. T4 bogies. dg. ETS 6X.

82301–305 converted 2008. 82306–308 converted 2011–12. 82309 converted 2013.

Fitted with a diesel generator for use while stabled in terminal stations or at depots. 48.5 t.

Lot No. 31042 Derby 1988. 45.2 t.

82301	(82117)	g	**CM**	AV	*CR*	AL
82302	(82151)	g	**CM**	AV	*CR*	AL
82303	(82135)	g	**CM**	AV	*CR*	AL
82304	(82130)	g	**CM**	AV	*CR*	AL
82305	(82134)	g	**CM**	AV	*CR*	AL
82306	(82144)		**AW**	DA	*RO*	RJ
82307	(82131)		**AW**	RO		BR
82308	(82108)		**AW**	RO		BR
82309	(82104)	g	**CM**	AV	*CR*	AL

GANGWAYED BRAKE VAN (100 mph)

Mark 1. Short frame (57 ft). Load 10 t. Adapted 199? for use as Brake Luggage Van. Guard's compartment retained and former baggage area adapted for secure stowage of passengers' luggage. B4 bogies. 100 mph. ETS 1X.

Lot No. 30162 Pressed Steel 1956–57. 30.5 t.

92904	(80867, 99554)	**VN**	WC	*WC*	CS

HIGH SECURITY GENERAL UTILITY VAN

Mark 1. Short frame (57 ft). Load 14 t. Modified with new floors, three roller shutter doors per side and the end doors removed. Commonwealth bogies. ETS 0X.

Lot No. 30616 Pressed Steel 1959–60. 32 t.

94225	(86849, 93849)	**M**	WC	*WC*	CS

GENERAL UTILITY VAN (100 mph)

Mark 1. Short frame (57 ft). Load 14 t. Screw couplers. Adapted 2013/201 for use as a water carrier with 3000 gallon capacity. ETS 0.

Non-standard livery: 96100 GWR Brown.

96100. Lot No. 30565 Pressed Steel 1959. 30 t. B5 bogies.
96175. Lot No. 30403 York/Glasgow 1958–60. 32 t. Commonwealth bogies

96100	(86734, 93734)	x	**0** VT	*VT*	TM
96175	(86628, 93628)	x	**M** WC	*WC*	CS

KITCHEN CAR

Mark 1 converted from Corridor First in 2008 with staff accommodation Commonwealth bogies. ETS 3.

Lot No. 30667 Swindon 1961. 35 t.

99316	(13321)	x	**M** WC	*WC*	CS

BUFFET STANDARD

Mark 1 converted from Open Standard in 2013 by the removal of two seatin bays and fitting of a buffet. –/48 2T. Commonwealth bogies. ETS 4.

Lot No. 30646 Wolverton 1961. 36 t.

99318	(4912)	x	**M** WC	*WC*	CS

KITCHEN CAR

Mark 1 converted from Corridor Standard in 2011 with staff accommodation Commonwealth bogies. ETS 3.

Lot No. 30685 Derby 1961–62. 34 t.

99712	(18893)	x	**M** WC	*WC*	CS

OPEN STANDARD

Mark 1 Corridor Standard rebuilt in 1997 as Open Standard using component from 4936. –/64 2T. Commonwealth bogies. ETS 4.

Lot No. 30685 Derby 1961–62. 36 t.

99722	(25806, 18806) x	**M**	WC	*WC*	CS

LUL 4 TC USED AS HAULED STOCK

The Class 438 4 TC sets were unpowered units designed to work in push pull mode with Class 430 (4 Rep) tractor units and Class 33/1, 73 and 74 locomotives. They were converted from locomotive-hauled coaching stock built 1952–57.

The vehicles listed are owned by London Underground and used on both special services on the LU Metropolitan Line and on occasional specials on the National Rail network, top-and-tailed by locomotives.

Mark 1. Trailer Brake Second side corridor with Lavatory (TBSK). Lot No. 30229. Metro-Cammell 1957. 35.5 t.

70823 (34970)   **M**   LU   *WC*   RS

Mark 1. Trailer First side corridor with Lavatory (TFK). Lot No. 30019. Swindon 1954. 33.5 t.

71163 (13097)   **M**   LU   *WC*   RS

Mark 1. Driving Trailer Second Open (DTSO).

76297. Lot No. 30086. Eastleigh 1955. 32.0 t.
76324. Lot No. 30149. Swindon 1956. 32.0 t.

76297 (3938)   **M**   LU   *WC*   RS
76324 (4009)   **M**   LU   *WC*   RS

NNR REGISTERED CARRIAGES

These carriages are permitted to operate on the national railway network only between Sheringham and Cromer as an extension of North Norfolk Railway (NNR) "North Norfolkman" services. Only NNR coaches currently registered for use on the national railway network are listed.

KITCHEN BUFFET STANDARD

Mark 1. Built as Unclassified Restaurant. Rebuilt with Buffet Counter and seating reduced. –/23. Commonwealth bogies. Lot No. 30632 Swindon 1960–61. 39 t.

1969   v   **CC**   NN   *NY*   NO

OPEN FIRST

Mark 1. 42/–. Commonwealth bogies. Lot No. 30697 Swindon 1962–63. 36 t.

116   v   **CC**   NN   *NY*   NO

OPEN STANDARD

Mark 1. –/48 2T. BR Mark 1 bogies. Lot No. 30121 Eastleigh 1953–55. 32 t.

372   v   **CC**   NN   *NY*   NO

GANGWAYED BRAKE VAN

Mark 1. Short frame (57 ft). Now fitted with a kitchen. BR Mark 1 bogies. Lot No. 30224 Cravens 1955–56. 31.5 t.

1033   v   **CC**   NN   *NY*   NO

NYMR REGISTERED CARRIAGES

These carriages are permitted to operate on the national railway network but may only be used to convey fare-paying passengers between Middlesbrough and Whitby on the Esk Valley branch as an extension of North Yorkshire Moors Railway services between Pickering and Grosmont. Only NYMR coaches currently registered for use on the national railway network are listed.

RESTAURANT FIRST

Mark 1. 24/–. Commonwealth bogies. Lot No. 30633 Swindon 1961. 42.5 t.

| 324 | x | **PC** | NY | *NY* | NY | JOS de CRAU |

BUFFET STANDARD

Mark 1. –/44 2T. Commonwealth bogies.
Lot No. 30520 Wolverton 1960. 38 t.

| 1823 | v | **M** | NY | *NY* | NY |

OPEN STANDARD

Mark 1. –/64 2T (* –/60 2W 2T, † –/60 3W 1T). BR Mark 1 bogies.
3798/3801. Lot No. 30079 York 1953. 33 t.
3860/72. Lot No. 30080 York 1954. 33 t.
3948. Lot No. 30086 Eastleigh 1954–55. 33 t.
4198/4252. Lot No. 30172 York 1956. 33 t.
4286/90. Lot No. 30207 BRCW 1956. 33 t.
4455. Lot No. 30226 BRCW 1957. 33 t.

3798	v	**M**	NY	*NY*	NY		4198	v*	**CC**	NY	*NY*	NY
3801	v	**CC**	NY	*NY*	NY		4252	v*	**CC**	NY	*NY*	NY
3860	v*	**M**	NY	*NY*	NY		4286	v	**CC**	NY	*NY*	NY
3872	v†	**BG**	NY	*NY*	NY		4290	v	**M**	NY	*NY*	NY
3948	v	**CC**	NY	*NY*	NY		4455	v	**CC**	NY	*NY*	NY

OPEN STANDARD

Mark 1. –/48 2T. BR Mark 1 bogies.
4786. Lot No. 30376 York 1957. 33 t.
4817. Lot No. 30473 BRCW 1959. 33 t.

| 4786 | v | **CH** | NY | *NY* | NY | | 4817 | v | **M** | NY | *NY* | NY |

OPEN STANDARD

Mark 1. Later vehicles built with Commonwealth bogies. –/64 2T.
Lot No. 30690 Wolverton 1961–62. Aluminium window frames. 37 t.

| 4990 | v | **M** | NY | *NY* | NY | | 5029 | v | **M** | NY | *NY* | NY |
| 5000 | v | **M** | NY | *NY* | NY | |

OPEN BRAKE STANDARD

Mark 1. –/39 1T. BR Mark 1 bogies.
Lot No. 30170 Doncaster 1956. 34 t.

| 225 | v | **M** | NY | *NY* | NY | | 9274 | v | **M** | NY | *NY* | NY |

CORRIDOR COMPOSITE

Mark 1. 24/18 1T. BR Mark 1 bogies.
5745. Lot No. 30179 Metro Cammell 1956. 36 t.
6156. Lot No. 30665 Derby 1961. 36 t.

| 5745 | v | **M** | NY | *NY* | NY | | 16156 | v | **CC** | NY | *NY* | NY |

CORRIDOR BRAKE COMPOSITE

Mark 1. Two First Class and three Standard Class compartments. 12/18 2T.
BR Mark 1 bogies.
Lot No. 30185 Metro Cammell 1956. 36 t.

| 1100 | v | **CC** | NY | *NY* | NY |

CORRIDOR BRAKE STANDARD

Mark 1. –/24 1T. BR Mark 1 bogies.
Lot No. 30233 Gloucester 1957. 35 t.

| 5089 | v | **CC** | NY | *NY* | NY |

PULLMAN BRAKE THIRD

Built 1928 by Metropolitan Carriage & Wagon Company. –/30. Gresley
bogies. 37.5 t.

| 32 | v | **PC** | NY | *NY* | NY | | CAR No. 79 |

PULLMAN KITCHEN FIRST

Built by Metro-Cammell 1960–61 for East Coast Main Line services. 20/– 2T.
Commonwealth bogies. 41.2 t.

| 318 | x | **PC** | NY | *NY* | NY | | ROBIN |

PULLMAN PARLOUR FIRST

Built by Metro-Cammell 1960–61 for East Coast Main Line services. 29/– 2T.
Commonwealth bogies. 38.5 t.

| 328 | x | **PC** | NY | *NY* | NY | | OPAL |

2. HIGH SPEED TRAIN TRAILER CARS

HSTs traditionally consist of a number of trailer cars (usually between four and nine) with a power car at each end. All trailers are classified Mark 3 and have BT10 bogies with disc brakes and central door locking. Heating is by a 415 V three-phase supply and vehicles have air conditioning. Maximum speed is 125 mph.

The trailer cars have one standard 23 m bodyshell for both First and Standard Class, thus facilitating easy conversion from one class to the other. As-built all cars had facing seating around tables with Standard Class carriages having nine bays of seats per side which did not line up with the eight windows per side.

All vehicles underwent a mid-life refurbishment in the 1980s with Standard Class seating layouts revised to incorporate unidirectional seating in addition to facing. A further refurbishment programme was completed in November 2000, with each company having a different scheme as follows:

Great Western Trains (later First Great Western). Green seat covers and extra partitions between seat bays.

Great North Eastern Railway. New lighting panels and brown seat covers.

Virgin CrossCountry. Green seat covers. Standard Class vehicles had four seats in the centre of each carriage replaced with a luggage stack.

Midland Mainline. Grey seat covers, redesigned seat squabs, side carpeting and two seats in the centre of each Standard Class carriage and one in First Class carriages replaced with a luggage stack.

Since then there have been many separate, and very different, projects:

Midland Mainline was first to refurbish its vehicles a second time in 2003–04. This involved fitting new fluorescent and halogen ceiling lighting although the original seats were retained, but with blue upholstery.

East Midlands Trains embarked on another, less radical, refurbishment in 2009–10 which included retention of the original seats but with red upholstery in Standard Class and blue in First. Subsequent operator East Midlands Railway used some former LNER rakes for a time before replacing all of its HSTs in 2021.

First Great Western (now Great Western Railway) started a major rebuild of its HST sets in late 2006, with the programme completed in 2008. The new interiors featured new lighting and seating throughout. First Class seats had leather upholstery, and were made by Primarius UK. Standard Class seats were of high-back design by Grammer. A number of sets operated without a full buffet or kitchen car, instead using one of 19 TS vehicles converted to include a "mini buffet" counter for use on shorter distance services. During 2012 15 402xx or 407xx buffet vehicles were converted to Trailer Standard to make the rakes formed as 7-cars up to 8-cars.

Many of the former GWR vehicles have now been scrapped, but GWR has retained 16 short 4-car sets for local and regional services. Trailers have been fitted with power doors and renumbered in the 48xxx and 49xxx series.

Having increased its sets to 9-car sets in 2004, at the end of 2006 **GNER** embarked on a major rebuild of its HSTs. All vehicles have similar interiors to the Mark 4 "Mallard" fleet, with new Primarius seating. The refurbishment of the 13 sets was completed by **National Express East Coast** in late 2009, these trains were later operated by **Virgin Trains East Coast** and then **London North Eastern Railway**. VTEC refurbished its sets in 2015–16, with the same seats retained but with new upholstery, and leather in First Class, but all sets were taken out of traffic with LNER by the end of 2019.

Open access operator **Grand Central** started operation in December 2007 with a new service from Sunderland to London King's Cross. This operator had three sets mostly using stock converted from loco-hauled Mark 3s. The seats in Standard Class have First Class spacing and in most vehicles are all facing. These sets were withdrawn in December 2017 and transferred to East Midlands Trains (now EMR). They were refurbished in 2018–19, with ex-GWR buffet cars used instead of the original Grand Central buffet cars.

CrossCountry reintroduced HSTs to the Cross-Country network from 2008. Five sets were refurbished at Wabtec, Doncaster principally for use on the Plymouth–Edinburgh route. Three of these sets use stock mostly converted from loco-hauled Mark 3s and two are sets ex-Midland Mainline. The interiors are similar to refurbished East Coast sets, although the seating layout is different and one toilet per carriage has been removed in favour of a luggage stack. These sets have now been fitted with sliding power doors.

ScotRail started operating HSTs from October 2018. The operator will have a fleet of 17 5-car and eight 4-car former GWR sets (fitted with sliding power doors) for use between Glasgow/Edinburgh and Aberdeen/Inverness, and on the Aberdeen–Inverness route.

Crewe-based **Locomotive Services** has acquired a number of former GWR and EMR HST vehicles and power cars. Two sets of First Class coaches are normally formed for charter use – one as the premium "Midland Pullman" in a striking blue livery and a second rake for Rail Charter Services in its green/silver livery. This latter set is used on regular services on the Settle & Carlisle line during the summer months. The **125 Group** also plans to return its rake of trailers and its power cars to the main line.

Operator Codes

Operator codes are shown in the heading before each set of vehicles. The first letter is always "T" for HST carriages, denoting a Trailer vehicle. The second letter denotes the passenger accommodation in that vehicle, for example "F" for First. "GS" denotes Guards accommodation and Standard Class seating. This is followed by catering provision, with "B" for buffet, and "K" for a kitchen and buffet:

TC	Trailer Composite	TGFB	Trailer Guard's Buffet First
TCK	Trailer Composite Kitchen	TSB	Trailer Buffet Standard
TF	Trailer First	TS	Trailer Standard
TFB	Trailer Buffet First	TGF	Trailer Guard's First
TFKB	Trailer Kitchen Buffet First	TGS	Trailer Guard's Standard

Power doors: All HSTs now operated by CrossCountry, Great Western Railway and ScotRail have been fitted with power sliding doors and retention toilets. Vehicles so fitted are shown with a "p" in the Notes column.

TRAILER BUFFET STANDARD   TSB

19 vehicles (40101–119) were converted at Laira 2009–10 from HST TSs fo
First Great Western. All other vehicles now scrapped. Grammer seating.

40106. Lot No. 30897 Derby 1977–79. –/70 1T. 35.5 t.

40106	(42162)	**FD**	LS		KR

TRAILER BUFFET FIRST   TFB

Converted from TSB by fitting First Class seats. Renumbered from 404x>
series by subtracting 200. Refurbished by First Great Western and fitte
with Primarius leather seating. 23/–.

40204–221. Lot No. 30883 Derby 1976–77. 36.12 t.

40204	**EA**	A		EP		40221	**EA**	A		EP
40205	**EA**	A		EP						

TRAILER GUARD'S MINIATURE BUFFET FIRST   TGFB

Refurbished 2018–21 for ScotRail. Former Great Western Railway vehicles
Primarius leather seating. Fitted with a new corner buffet counter and
kitchen. 32/– 1T.

40601–626. For Lot No. details see TF. 39.1 t.

40601	(41032)	p	**SI**	A	*SR*	IS		40614	(41010)	p	**SI**	A	*SR*	IS
40602	(41038)	p	**SI**	A	*SR*	IS		40615	(41022)	p	**SI**	A	*SR*	IS
40603	(41006)	p	**SI**	A	*SR*	IS		40616	(41142)	p	**SI**	A	*SR*	IS
40604	(41024)	p	**SI**	A	*SR*	IS		40617	(41144)	p	**SI**	A	*SR*	IS
40605	(41094)	p	**SI**	A	*SR*	IS		40618	(41016)	p	**SI**	A	*SR*	IS
40606	(41104)	p	**SI**	A	*SR*	IS		40619	(41124)	p	**SI**	A	*SR*	IS
40607	(41136)	p	**SI**	A	*SR*	IS		40620	(41158)	p	**SI**	A	*SR*	IS
40608	(41122)	p	**SI**	A	*SR*	IS		40621	(41146)	p	**SI**	A	*SR*	IS
40609	(41020)	p	**SI**	A	*SR*	IS		40623	(41180)	p	**SI**	A	*SR*	IS
40610	(41103)	p	**SI**	A	*SR*	IS		40624	(41116)	p	**SI**	A	*SR*	IS
40611	(41130)	p	**SI**	A	*SR*	IS		40625	(41137)	p	**SI**	A	*SR*	IS
40612	(41134)	p	**SI**	A	*SR*	IS		40626	(41012)	p	**SI**	A	*SR*	IS
40613	(41135)	p	**SI**	A	*SR*	IS								

TRAILER KITCHEN BUFFET FIRST   TFKB

These vehicles have larger kitchens than the 402xx and 404xx series
vehicles, and are used in trains where a full meal service is required
They were renumbered from the 403xx series (in which the seats were
unclassified) by adding 400 to the previous number. 17/–.

* Refurbished former GWR vehicles. Primarius leather seating.
m Refurbished former LNER vehicles with Primarius leather seating.

40704–720. Lot No. 30921 Derby 1978–79. 38.16 t.
40728–734. Lot No. 30940 Derby 1979–80. 38.16 t.
40750. Lot No. 30948 Derby 1980–81. 38.16 t.
40755. Lot No. 30966 Derby 1982. 38.16 t.

40704	m	**VE**	A		EP	40734	*	**FD**	A		EP
40715	*	**GW**	A		EP	40741		**ST**	125		RD
40720	m	**BG**	A		EP	40750	m	**VE**	A	*EM*	NL
40728		**ST**	125		RD	40755	*	**GW**	A		ZG
40730		**ST**	DA	*RO*	RJ						

TRAILER KITCHEN BUFFET FIRST TFKB

These vehicles have been converted from TSBs in the 404xx series to be similar to the 407xx series vehicles. 17/–. Primarius leather seating.

40802 and 40804 were numbered 40212 and 40232 for a time when fitted with 23 First Class seats.

40801/802/808. Lot No. 30883 Derby 1976–77. 38.16 t.
40804. Lot No. 30899 Derby 1978–79. 38.16 t.

40801	(40027, 40427)	**MP**	LS	*LS*	CL
40802	(40012, 40412)	**MP**	LS	*LS*	CL
40804	(40032, 40432)	**RC**	LS	*LS*	CL
40808	(40015, 40415)	**FD**	LS		KR

TRAILER BUFFET FIRST TFB

Converted from TSB by First Great Western. Refurbished with Primarius leather seating. 23/–.

40900/902/904. Lot No. 30883 Derby 1976–77. 36.12 t.

40900	(40022, 40422)	**FD**	FG		LM
40902	(40023, 40423)	**FD**	FG		LM
40904	(40001, 40401)	**GW**	FG		LM

TRAILER FIRST TF

As built and m 48/– 2T (m† 48/– 1T – one toilet removed for trolley space).
* Refurbished former GWR vehicles. Primarius leather seating.
n Refurbished former LNER vehicles with Primarius leather seating.
x Refurbished CrossCountry vehicles with power doors, Primarius seating and one toilet removed. 39/– 1TD 1W.
t Fitted with centre luggage stack, disabled toilet and wheelchair space. 46/– 1TD 1T 1W.
v Wheelchair space. 47/– 2T 1W.

41026/035. Lot No. 30881 Derby 1976–77. 33.66 t.
41057–118. Lot No. 30896 Derby 1977–78. 33.66 t.
41149–166. Lot No. 30947 Derby 1980. 33.66 t.
41167/169. Lot No. 30963 Derby 1982. 33.66 t.
41170. Lot No. 30967 Derby 1982. Former prototype vehicle. 33.66 t.

41176. Lot No. 30897 Derby 1977. 33.66 t.
41182/183. Lot No. 30939 Derby 1979–80. 33.66 t.
41187. Lot No. 30969 Derby 1982. 33.66 t.
41193–195/204–206. Lot No. 30878 Derby 1975–76. 34.3 t. Converted from Mark 3A Open First.
41208/209. Lot No. 30877 Derby 1975–77. Converted from Mark 3A Ope Standard.

41026	px	**XC**	A	*XC*	LA		41108	*w	**MP**	LS	*LS*	CL
41035	px	**XC**	A	*XC*	LA		41117		**ST**	LS	*LS*	CL
41057		**ST**	125		RD		41118	mw	**BG**	A		EP
41059	*w	**MP**	LS	*LS*	CL		41149	*w	**GW**	LS		KR
41063		**ST**	LS	*LS*	CL		41160	*w	**RC**	LS	*LS*	CL
41067	s	**ST**	125		RD		41162	*w	**MP**	LS	*LS*	CL
41087	mt	**VE**	A		EP		41165	mw	**VE**	P		BU
41091	mt	**VE**	A		EP		41166	*w	**RC**	LS	*LS*	CL
41100	mw	**VE**	A		EP		41167	*w	**FD**	LS		ZG
41106	*w	**FD**	A		ZG		41169	*w	**MP**	LS	*LS*	CL

41170	(41001)		mt	**BG**	A	EP
41176	(42142, 42352)		*w	**MP**	LS *LS*	CL
41182	(42278)		*w	**MP**	LS *LS*	CL
41183	(42274)		*w	**MP**	LS *LS*	CL
41187	(42311)		*w	**RC**	LS *LS*	CL

The following carriages have been converted from loco-hauled Mark 3 vehicles

41193	(11060)		px	**XC**	P	*XC*	LA
41194	(11016)		px	**XC**	P	*XC*	LA
41195	(11020)		px	**XC**	P	*XC*	LA
41204	(11023)			**EA**	A		EP
41205	(11036)		w	**EA**	A		EP
41206	(11055)			**EA**	A		EP
41208	(12112, 42406)		w	**EA**	A		EP
41209	(12088, 42409)			**EA**	A		EP

TRAILER STANDARD   TS

42310 was numbered 41188 for a time when fitted with First Class seats.

Standard seating and m –/76 2T.
* Refurbished former Great Western Railway vehicles. Grammer seating. –/80 2T (unless h – high density).
h "High density" former Great Western Railway vehicles. –/84 2T.
k "High density" former Great Western Railway refurbished vehicle with disabled persons toilet and 5, 6 or 7 tip-up seats. –/72 1T 1TD 2W.
m Refurbished former LNER vehicles with Primarius seating.
pr Refurbished ScotRail vehicles with power doors and Grammer seating. –/74
ps Refurbished ScotRail vehicles with power doors and Grammer seating. –/74
p* Refurbished ScotRail vehicles with power doors, Grammer seating and universal access toilet. –/58 1TD 2W.
px Refurbished CrossCountry vehicles with power doors and Primarius seating. –/80 1T.

† Refurbished CrossCountry vehicles with power doors, Primarius seating and universal access toilet. –/64 1TD 2W.
Centre luggage stack (EMR) –/74 2T.
∕ Centre luggage stack and wheelchair space (EMR) –72 2T 1W.
Disabled persons toilet (LNER) –/62 1T 1TD 1W.

2004–078. Lot No. 30882 Derby 1976–77. 33.6 t.
2094–250. Lot No. 30897 Derby 1977–79. 33.6 t.
2252–301. Lot No. 30939 Derby 1979–80. 33.6 t.
2310/319. Lot No. 30969 Derby 1982. 33.6 t.
2325–337. Lot No. 30983 Derby 1984–85. 33.6 t.
2342/360. Lot No. 30949 Derby 1982. 33.47 t. Converted from TGS.
2343/345. Lot No. 30970 Derby 1982. 33.47 t. Converted from TGS.
2347/350/351/379/380/551–563. Lot No. 30881 Derby 1976–77. 33.66 t. onverted from TF.
2353/355/357. Lot No. 30967 Derby 1982. Ex-prototype vehicles. 33.66 t.
2363/565–569. Lot No. 30896 Derby 1977–78. 33.66 t. Converted from TF.
2366–378/401–408. Lot No. 30877 Derby 1975–77. 34.3 t. Converted from Mark 3A Open Standard.
2503. Lot No. 30921 Derby 1978–79. 34.8 t. Converted from TFKB.
2506. Lot No. 30940 Derby 1979–80. 34.8 t. Converted from TFKB.
2571–579. Lot No. 30938 Derby 1979–80. 33.66 t. Converted from TF.
2581/583. Lot No. 30947 Derby 1980. 33.66 t. Converted from TF.
2584/585. Lot No. 30878 Derby 1975–76. Converted from Mark 3A Open First.

2004	p*	SI	A	SR	IS	42055	p*	SI	A	SR	IS
2009	ps	SI	A	SR	IS	42056	ps	SI	A	SR	IS
2010	ps	SI	A	SR	IS	42072	pr	SI	A	SR	IS
2012	p*	SI	A	SR	IS	42075	ps	SI	A	SR	IS
2013	ps	SI	A	SR	IS	42077	ps	SI	A	SR	IS
2014	ps	SI	A	SR	IS	42078	ps	SI	A	SR	IS
2019	ps	SI	A	SR	IS	42094	*h	FD	FG		LA
2021	p*	SI	A	SR	IS	42095	*	FD	FG		LA
2023	ps	SI	A	SR	IS	42096	ps	SI	A	SR	IS
2024	*k	FD			EP	42097	px	XC	A	XC	LA
2028	*h	FD			EP	42100	u	ST	LS	LS	CL
2029	ps	SI	A	SR	IS	42107	pr	SI	A	SR	IS
2030	p*	SI	A	SR	IS	42109	m	VE	P		BU
2032	ps	SI	A	SR	IS	42110	m	VE	NS		BU
2033	ps	SI	A	SR	IS	42111	u	ST	125		RD
2034	pr	SI	A	SR	IS	42119	u	ST	125		RD
2035	ps	SI	A	SR	IS	42120	u	ST	125		RD
2036	px	XC	A	XC	LA	42129	ps	SI	A	SR	IS
2037	px	XC	A	XC	LA	42143	ps	SI	A	SR	IS
2038	px	XC	A	XC	LA	42144	ps	SI	A	SR	IS
2045	ps	SI	A	SR	IS	42167	*h	FD	FG		LM
2046	ps	SI	A	SR	IS	42173	*k	FD	GW		ZB
2047	ps	SI	A	SR	IS	42175	*h	FD	FG		LA
2051	px	XC	A	XC	LA	42176	*h	FD	P		LM
2052	px	XC	A	XC	LA	42179	m	VE	A		EP
2053	px	XC	A	XC	LA	42183	p*	SI	A	SR	IS
2054	ps	SI	A	SR	IS	42184	ps	SI	A	SR	IS

42185	ps	**SI**	A	*SR*	IS
42195	*k	**FD**	GW		ZB
42200	p*	**SI**	A	*SR*	IS
42206	p*	**SI**	A	*SR*	IS
42207	p*	**SI**	A	*SR*	IS
42208	p*	**SI**	A	*SR*	IS
42209	ps	**SI**	A	*SR*	IS
42213	ps	**SI**	A	*SR*	IS
42217	*k	**FD**	GW		ZB
42220	w	**ST**	LS	*LS*	CL
42231	*h	**FD**	FG		LM
42234	px	**XC**	P	*XC*	LA
42242	m	**BG**	A		EP
42243	m	**BG**	A		EP
42245	pr	**SI**	A	*SR*	IS
42250	ps	**SI**	A	*SR*	IS
42252	ps	**SI**	A	*SR*	IS
42253	p*	**SI**	A	*SR*	IS
42255	p*	**SI**	A	*SR*	IS
42256	ps	**SI**	A	*SR*	IS
42257	ps	**SI**	A	*SR*	IS
42259	p*	**SI**	A	*SR*	IS
42265	p*	**SI**	A	*SR*	IS
42267	p*	**SI**	A	*SR*	IS
42268	p*	**SI**	A	*SR*	IS
42269	ps	**SI**	A	*SR*	IS
42275	p*	**SI**	A	*SR*	IS
42276	ps	**SI**	A	*SR*	IS
42277	ps	**SI**	A	*SR*	IS
42279	p*	**SI**	A	*SR*	IS
42280	pr	**SI**	A	*SR*	IS
42281	p*	**SI**	A	*SR*	IS
42288	ps	**SI**	A	*SR*	IS
42290	px	**XC**	P	*XC*	LA
42291	p*	**SI**	A	*SR*	IS
42292	p*	**SI**	A	*SR*	IS
42293	ps	**SI**	A	*SR*	IS
42295	p*	**SI**	A	*SR*	IS
42296	ps	**SI**	A	*SR*	IS
42297	p*	**SI**	A	*SR*	IS
42299	p*	**SI**	A	*SR*	IS
42300	pr	**SI**	A	*SR*	IS
42301	ps	**SI**	A	*SR*	IS
42310	*k	**FD**	GW		ZB
42319	*h	**GW**	LS		KR
42325	pr	**SI**	A	*SR*	IS
42333	ps	**SI**	A	*SR*	IS
42337	w	**ST**	125		RD

42342	(44082)		px	**XC**	A	*XC*	LA
42343	(44095)		ps	**SI**	A	*SR*	IS
42345	(44096)		p*	**SI**	A	*SR*	IS
42347	(41054)		*k	**FD**	A		EP
42350	(41047)		ps	**SI**	A	*SR*	IS
42351	(41048)		ps	**SI**	A	*SR*	IS
42353	(42001, 41171)		*k	**FD**	GW		ZB
42355	(42000, 41172)		m	**VE**	A		EP
42357	(41002, 41174)		m	**VE**	A		EP
42360	(44084, 45084)		p*	**SI**	A	*SR*	IS
42363	(41082)		mt	**BG**	A		EP

42366–378 were converted from loco-hauled Mark 3 vehicles for CrossCountry

42366	(12007)	pt	**XC**	P	*XC*	LA
42367	(12025)	px	**XC**	P	*XC*	LA
42368	(12028)	px	**XC**	P	*XC*	LA
42369	(12050)	px	**XC**	P	*XC*	LA
42370	(12086)	px	**XC**	P	*XC*	LA
42371	(12052)	pt	**XC**	P	*XC*	LA
42372	(12055)	px	**XC**	P	*XC*	LA
42373	(12071)	px	**XC**	P	*XC*	LA
42374	(12075)	pt	**XC**	P	*XC*	LA
42375	(12113)	px	**XC**	P	*XC*	LA
42376	(12085)	pt	**XC**	P	*XC*	LA
42377	(12102)	px	**XC**	P	*XC*	LA
42378	(12123)	px	**XC**	P	*XC*	LA

| 42379 | (41036) | p† **XC** | A | *XC* | LA |
| 42380 | (41025) | p† **XC** | A | *XC* | LA |

These carriages were converted from loco-hauled Mark 3 vehicles for Grand Central. They have a lower density seating layout (most seats arranged round tables). –/62 2T.

42401	(12149)	**EA**	A		EP
42402	(12155)	**EA**	A		EP
42404	(12152)	**EA**	A		EP
42405	(12136)	**EA**	A		EP
42408	(12121)	**EA**	A		EP

These carriages were converted from TFKB or TSB buffet cars to TS vehicles in 2011–12 at Wabtec Kilmarnock for FGW. Refurbished with Grammer seating. –/84 1T. 34.8 t.

| 42503 | (40312, 40712) | **FD** | WA | | ZB |
| 42506 | (40324, 40724) | **FD** | A | | EP |

These carriages were converted from TF to TS vehicles in 2014 at Wabtec Kilmarnock for FGW. Refurbished with Grammer seating. –/80 1T (pr –/74). 35.5 t.

42551	(41003)	pr **SI**	A	*SR*	IS
42553	(41009)	pr **SI**	A	*SR*	IS
42555	(41015)	pr **SI**	A	*SR*	IS
42557	(41019)	pr **SI**	A	*SR*	IS
42558	(41021)	pr **SI**	A	*SR*	IS
42559	(41023)	pr **SI**	A	*SR*	IS
42561	(41031)	pr **SI**	A	*SR*	IS
42562	(41037)	pr **SI**	A	*SR*	IS
42563	(41045)	**FD**	FG		LM
42565	(41085)	**FD**	FG		LM
42566	(41086)	**FD**	FG		PZ
42567	(41093)	pr **SI**	A	*SR*	IS
42568	(41101)	pr **SI**	A	*SR*	IS
42569	(41105)	**FD**	A		EP
42571	(41121)	pr **SI**	A	*SR*	IS
42574	(41129)	pr **SI**	A	*SR*	IS
42575	(41131)	pr **SI**	A	*SR*	IS
42576	(41133)	pr **SI**	A	*SR*	IS
42577	(41141)	pr **SI**	A	*SR*	IS
42578	(41143)	pr **SI**	A	*SR*	IS
42579	(41145)	pr **SI**	A	*SR*	IS
42581	(41157)	pr **SI**	A	*SR*	IS
42583	(41153, 42385)	**GW**	LS		KR

These carriages were converted from loco-hauled carriages for Grand Central, before being converted to TS for East Midlands Railway. –/62 2T.

| 42584 | (11045, 41201) | **EA** | A | | EP |
| 42585 | (11017, 41202) | **EA** | A | | EP |

TRAILER GUARD'S STANDARD/FIRST   TGS/TGF

As built and m –/65 1T.
* Refurbished Great Western Railway vehicles. Grammer seating and
  toilet removed for trolley store. –/67 (unless h).
† Converted to Trailer Guard's First (TGF) with Primarius seating. 36/–.
p Refurbished CrossCountry vehicles with power doors and Primarius
  seating. –/67.
h "High density" Great Western Railway vehicles. –/71.
m Refurbished former LNER vehicles with Primarius seating.
s Fitted with centre luggage stack (EMR) –/63 1T.
t Fitted with centre luggage stack –/61 1T.

44000. Lot No. 30953 Derby 1980. 33.47 t.
44004–089. Lot No. 30949 Derby 1980–82. 33.47 t.
44094. Lot No. 30964 Derby 1982. 33.47 t.
44098/100. Lot No. 30970 Derby 1982. 33.47 t.

44000	*h	**GW**	125		RD	44061	m	**VE**	A		EP
44004	*h	**FD**	WA		ZB	44063	m	**VE**	A		EP
44012	p	**XC**	A	*XC*	LA	44066	*	**FD**	WA		ZB
44017	p	**XC**	A	*XC*	LA	44072	p	**XC**	P	*XC*	LA
44020	*h	**FD**	WA		ZB	44078	†	**MP**	LS	*LS*	CL
44021	p	**XC**	P	*XC*	LA	44081	†	**RC**	LS	*LS*	CL
44024	*h	**FD**	WA		ZB	44086	*	**GW**	WA		ZB
44034	*	**FD**	A		EP	44089	t	**V**	ER		ZR
44035	*	**FD**	WA		ZB	44094	m	**VE**	A		EP
44040	*	**GW**	WA		ZB	44098	m	**BG**	A		EP
44047	s	**ST**	LS	*LS*	CL	44100	*h	**FD**	P		PZ
44052	p	**XC**	P	*XC*	LA						

TRAILER COMPOSITE KITCHEN   TCK

Converted from Mark 3A Open Standard. Refurbished CrossCountry
vehicles with Primarius seating. Small kitchen for the preparation of hot
food and stowage space for two trolleys between First and Standard Class.
One toilet removed. 30/8 1T.

45001–005. Lot No. 30877 Derby 1975–77. 34.3 t.

45001	(12004)	p	**XC**	P	*XC*	LA
45002	(12106)	p	**XC**	P	*XC*	LA
45003	(12076)	p	**XC**	P	*XC*	LA
45004	(12077)	p	**XC**	P	*XC*	LA
45005	(12080)	p	**XC**	P	*XC*	LA

TRAILER COMPOSITE   TC

Converted from TF for First Great Western 2014–15. Refurbished with
Grammer seating. 24/39 1T.

46006. Lot No. 30896 Derby 1977–78. 35.6 t. Converted from TF.
46012. Lot No. 30938 Derby 1979–80. 35.6 t. Converted from TF.
46014. Lot No. 30963 Derby 1982. 35.6 t. Converted from TF.

46006	(41081)	**FD**	LS	ZG
46012	(41147)	**FD**	LS	KR
46014	(41168)	**FD**	LS	ZG

TRAILER STANDARD   TS

Refurbished for Great Western Railway 2017–21 and fitted with power doors
and retention toilets. Used in 4-car sets on local and regional services
across the South-West. –/84 1T († –/62 + 5 tip-ups 1TD 2W).

48101–137/140–150. For Lot No. details see TS. 36.3 t.

48101	(42093, 48111)	p	**GW**	FG	*GW*	LA
48102	(42218)	p†	**GW**	FG	*GW*	LA
48103	(42168, 48101)	p	**GW**	FG	*GW*	LA
48104	(41107, 42365)	p	**GW**	FG	*GW*	LA
48105	(42266)	p†	**GW**	FG	*GW*	LA
48106	(42258)	p	**GW**	FG	*GW*	LA
48107	(42101)	p	**GW**	FG	*GW*	LA
48108	(42174)	p†	**GW**	FG	*GW*	LA
48109	(42085)	p	**GW**	FG	*GW*	LA
48110	(42315)	p	**GW**	FG	*GW*	LA
48111	(42224)	p†	**GW**	FG	*GW*	LA
48112	(42222)	p	**GW**	FG	*GW*	LA
48113	(42177, 48102)	p	**GW**	FG	*GW*	LA
48114	(42317)	p†	**GW**	FG	*GW*	LA
48115	(42285)	p	**GW**	A	*GW*	LA
48116	(42273)	p	**GW**	A	*GW*	LA
48117	(42271)	p†	**GW**	A	*GW*	LA
48118	(42073)	p	**GW**	A	*GW*	LA
48119	(42204)	p	**GW**	A	*GW*	LA
48120	(42201)	p†	**GW**	A	*GW*	LA
48121	(42027)	p	**GW**	A	*GW*	LA
48122	(42214)	p	**GW**	A	*GW*	LA
48123	(42211)	p†	**GW**	A	*GW*	LA
48124	(42212)	p	**GW**	A	*GW*	LA
48125	(42203)	p	**GW**	A	*GW*	LA
48126	(42138)	p†	**GW**	A	*GW*	LA
48127	(42349)	p	**GW**	A	*GW*	LA
48128	(42044)	p	**GW**	A	*GW*	LA
48129	(42008)	p†	**GW**	A	*GW*	LA
48130	(42102, 48131)	p	**GW**	FG	*GW*	LA

48131	(42042)	p	**GW**	A	*GW*	LA
48132	(42202)	p†	**GW**	A	*GW*	LA
48133	(42003)	p	**GW**	A	*GW*	LA
48134	(42264)	p†	**GW**	A	*GW*	LA
48135	(42251)	p†	**GW**	A	*GW*	LA
48136	(41114, 42570)	p	**GW**	FG	*GW*	LA
48137	(41163, 42582)	p	**GW**	FG	*GW*	LA
48140	(42005)	p	**GW**	GW	*GW*	LA
48141	(42015)	p†	**GW**	GW	*GW*	LA
48142	(42016)	p	**GW**	GW	*GW*	LA
48143	(42050)	p	**GW**	GW	*GW*	LA
48144	(42066)	p†	**GW**	GW	*GW*	LA
48145	(42048)	p	**GW**	GW	*GW*	LA
48146	(42074)	p	**GW**	GW	*GW*	LA
48147	(42081)	p†	**GW**	GW	*GW*	LA
48148	(42071)	p	**GW**	GW	*GW*	LA
48149	(42087)	p	**GW**	GW	*GW*	LA
48150	(42580)	p	**GW**	GW	*GW*	LA

TRAILER GUARD'S STANDARD   TG

Refurbished for Great Western Railway 2017–21 and fitted with powe
doors. –/71.

49101–117. For Lot No. details see TGS. 35.7 t.

49101	(44055)	p	**GW**	FG	*GW*	LA
49102	(44083)	p	**GW**	FG	*GW*	LA
49103	(44097)	p	**GW**	FG	*GW*	LA
49104	(44101)	p	**GW**	FG	*GW*	LA
49105	(44090)	p	**GW**	FG	*GW*	LA
49106	(44033)	p	**GW**	A	*GW*	LA
49107	(44064)	p	**GW**	A	*GW*	LA
49108	(44067)	p	**GW**	A	*GW*	LA
49109	(44003)	p	**GW**	A	*GW*	LA
49110	(44014)	p	**GW**	A	*GW*	LA
49111	(44036)	p	**GW**	A	*GW*	LA
49112	(44079)	p	**GW**	FG	*GW*	LA
49113	(44008)	p	**GW**	A	*GW*	LA
49114	(44005)	p	**GW**	GW	*GW*	LA
49115	(44016)	p	**GW**	GW	*GW*	LA
49116	(44002)	p	**GW**	GW	*GW*	LA
49117	(44042)	p	**GW**	GW	*GW*	LA

HST SET FORMATIONS

GREAT WESTERN RAILWAY

GWR has retained and refurbished 16 4-car sets for use on regional and local services in the South-West.

Number of sets: 16.   **Maximum number of daily diagrams:** 12.
Formations: 4-cars.   **Allocation:** Laira (Plymouth).
Other maintenance and servicing depots: Long Rock (Penzance), St Philip's Marsh (Bristol).
Operation: Bristol–Exeter–Plymouth–Penzance and Cardiff–Bristol–Taunton

Set	D	C	B	A
GW01	48103	48102	48101	49101
GW02	48106	48105	48104	49102
GW03	48109	48108	48107	49103
GW04	48112	48111	48110	49104
GW05	48115	48114	48113	49105
GW06	48118	48117	48116	49106
GW07	48121	48120	48119	49107
GW08	48124	48123	48122	49108
GW09	48127	48126	48125	49109
GW10	48130	48129	48128	49110
GW11	48133	48132	48131	49111
GW12	48136	48135	48134	49112
GW13	48150	48149	48137	49113
GW14	48142	48141	48140	49114
GW15	48145	48144	48143	49115
GW16	48148	48147	48146	49116

Spare:

LA: 49117

CROSSCOUNTRY

CrossCountry HSTs run in 7-car formation. All are fitted with power doors

Number of sets: 5.   **Maximum number of daily diagrams:** 4.
Formations: 7-cars.   **Allocation:** Laira (Plymouth).
Other maintenance depots: Neville Hill (Leeds) or Edinburgh (Craigentinny
Operation: Edinburgh–Leeds–Plymouth is the core route.

Set	A	B	C	D	E	F	G
XC01	41193	45001	42342	42097	42377	42380	44021
XC02	41194	45002	42053	42037	42234	42371	44072
XC03	41195	45003	42375	42378	42036	42376	44052
XC04	41026	45004	42290	42369	42038	42366	44012
XC05	41035	45005	42373	42368	42370	42379	44017

Spares:

LA: 42051   42052   42367   42372   42374

SCOTRAIL

ScotRail is introducing refurbished HSTs onto its Edinburgh/Glasgow–Aberdeen/Inverness services – branded INTER-7-CITY as they serve Scotland's seven cities. There will ultimately be 17 5-car and eight 4-car sets (HA22 was written off in the 2020 Carmont accident). The first 5-car sets were introduced in autumn 2021 and further 4-cars sets will be lengthened to 5-cars during 2021–22.

Number of sets: 25.
Number of diagrams as at autumn 2021: 11.
Formations: 4-cars or 5-cars.
Allocation: Power cars: Haymarket (Edinburgh), Trailers: Inverness.
Operation: Edinburgh/Glasgow–Aberdeen, Edinburgh/Glasgow–Inverness, Aberdeen–Inverness.

Set	A	B	C	D	E
HA01	40601	42004	42561	42046	
HA02	40602	42292	42562	42045	
HA03	40603	42021	42557	42143	
HA04	40604	42183	42559	42343	
HA05	40605	42345	42034	42184	
HA06	40606	42206	42581	42208	
HA07	40607	42207	42574	42288	
HA08	40608	42055	42571	42019	
HA09	40609	42253	42107	42257	
HA10	40610	42360	42551	42252	42351
HA11	40611	42267	42325	42301	42023
HA12	40612	42275	42576	42276	
HA13	40613	42279	42280	42296	
HA14	40614	42012	42245	42013	
HA15	40615	42030	42579	42010	
HA16	40616	42291	42577	42075	
HA17	40617	42295	42558	42250	
HA18	40618	42297	42555	42014	
HA19	40619	42255	42568	42256	
HA20	40620	42200	42575	42129	
HA21	40621	42299	42300	42277	
HA22	40623	42268	42567	42269	
HA24	40624	42265	42553	42293	
HA25	40625	42259	42578	42333	
HA26	40626	42281	42072	42350	

Extra coaches to make further sets up to 5-car rakes:

42009 42029 42032 42033 42035 42047 42054 42056 42077
42078 42096 42144 42185 42209 42213

3. SALOONS

Several specialist passenger carrying carriages, normally referred to a saloons are permitted to run on the national railway system. Many of thes are to pre-nationalisation designs.

WCJS FIRST CLASS SALOON

Built 1892 by LNWR, Wolverton. Originally dining saloon mounted on si wheel bogies. Rebuilt with new underframe with four-wheel bogies in 192 Rebuilt 1960 as observation saloon with DMU end. Gangwayed at oth end. The interior has a saloon, kitchen, guards vestibule and observatio lounge. 19/– 1T. Gresley bogies. 28.5 t. 75 mph. ETS x.

41   (484, 45018) x   **M**   WC   *WC*   CS

LNWR DINING SALOON

Built 1890 by LNWR, Wolverton. Mounted on the underframe of LM General Utility Van 37908 in the 1980s. Contains kitchen and dining are seating 12 at tables for two. 12/–. Gresley bogies. 75 mph. 25.4 t. ETS x.

159   (5159)   x   **M**   WC   *WC*   CS

GNR FIRST CLASS SALOON

Built 1912 by GNR, Doncaster. Contains entrance vestibule, lavatory, tw separate saloons, library and luggage space. 19/– 1T. Gresley bogie 75 mph. 29.4 t. ETS x.

Non-standard livery: Teak.

807   (4807)   x   **0**   WC   *WC*   CS

LNER GENERAL MANAGERS SALOON

Built 1945 by LNER, York. Gangwayed at one end with a veranda at th other. The interior has a dining saloon seating 12, kitchen, toilet, office an nine seat lounge. 21/– 1T. B4 bogies. 75 mph. 35.7 t. ETS 3.

1999   (902260)   **M**   WC   CS   DINING CAR No. 2

GENERAL MANAGER'S SALOON

Renumbered 1989 from London Midland Region departmental series. Formerly the LMR General Manager's saloon. Rebuilt from LMS period 1 Corridor Brake First M5033M to dia 1654 and mounted on the underframe of BR suburban Brake Standard M43232. Screw couplings have been removed. B4 bogies. 100 mph. ETS 2X.

LMS Lot No. 326 Derby 1927. 27.5 t.

5320 (5033, DM 395707) x **M** PR *PR* SK

SUPPORT CAR

Converted 199? from Courier vehicle converted from Mark 1 Corridor Brake Standard 1986–87. Toilet retained and former compartment area replaced with train manager's office, crew locker room, linen store and dry goods store. The former luggage area has been adapted for use as an engineers' compartment and workshop. B5 bogies. 100 mph. ETS 2.

Lot No. 30721 Wolverton 1963. 35.5 t.

99545 (35466, 80207) **PC** BE *BP* SL BAGGAGE CAR No. 11

SERVICE CAR

Converted from BR Mark 1 Corridor Brake Standard. Commonwealth bogies. 100 mph. ETS 2.

Lot No. 30721 Wolverton 1963.

99886 (35407) x **M** WC *WC* CS 86 SERVICE CAR No. 1

ROYAL SCOTSMAN SALOONS

Built 1960 by Metro-Cammell as Pullman Kitchen Second for East Coast Main Line Services. Rebuilt 2016 as a Spa Car with two large bedrooms with bathroom/spa areas. Commonwealth bogies. xx t. ETS ?.

99337 (CAR No. 337) **M** BE *RS* HN STATE SPA CAR

Built 1960 by Metro-Cammell as Pullman Kitchen First for East Coast Main Line services. Rebuilt 2013 as dining car. Commonwealth bogies. 38.5 t. ETS ?.

99960 (321 SWIFT) **M** BE *RS* HN DINING CAR No. 2

Built 1960 by Metro-Cammell as Pullman Parlour First (§ Pullman Kitchen First) for East Coast Main Line services. Rebuilt 1990 as sleeping cars with four twin sleeping rooms (*§ three twin sleeping rooms and two single sleeping rooms at each end). Commonwealth bogies. 38.5 t. ETS ?.

99961	(324 AMBER) *	**M**	BE	*RS*	HN	STATE CAR No. 1
99962	(329 PEARL)	**M**	BE	*RS*	HN	STATE CAR No. 2
99963	(331 TOPAZ)	**M**	BE	*RS*	HN	STATE CAR No. 3
99964	(313 FINCH) §	**M**	BE	*RS*	HN	STATE CAR No. 4

Built 1960 by Metro-Cammell as Pullman Kitchen First for East Coast Main Line services. Rebuilt 1990 as observation car with open verandah seating 32. B4 bogies. 36.95 t. ETS ?.

| 99965 | (319 SNIPE) | **M** | BE | *RS* | HN | OBSERVATION CAR |

Built 1960 by Metro-Cammell as Pullman Kitchen First for East Coast Main Line services. Rebuilt 1993 as dining car. Commonwealth bogies. 38.5 t ETS ?.

| 99967 | (317 RAVEN) | **M** | BE | *RS* | HN | DINING CAR No. 1 |

Mark 3A. Converted 1997 from a Sleeping Car at Carnforth Railway Restoration & Engineering Services. BT10 bogies. Attendant's and adjacent two sleeping compartments converted to generator room containing a 160 kW Volvo unit. In 99968 four sleeping compartments remain for staff use with another converted for use as a staff shower and toilet. The remaining five sleeping compartments have been replaced by two passenger cabins. In 99969 seven sleeping compartments remain for staff use. A further sleeping compartment along with one toilet, have been converted to store rooms. The other two sleeping compartments have been combined to form a crew mess. 41.5 t. 99968 ETS index ?. 99969 ETS 7X (when generator not in use). ETS index ? (when generator in use).

Lot No. 30960 Derby 1981–83.

| 99968 | (10541) | **M** | BE | *RS* | HN | STATE CAR No. 5 |
| 99969 | (10556) | **M** | BE | *RS* | HN | SERVICE CAR |

"CLUB CAR"

Converted from BR Mark 1 Open Standard at Carnforth Railway Restoration & Engineering Services in 1994. Contains kitchen, pantry and two dining saloons. 20/– 1T. Commonwealth bogies. 100 mph. ETS 4.

Lot No. 30724 York 1963. 37 t.

| 99993 | (5067) | x | **CC** | LS | *LS* | CL | CLUB CAR |

BR INSPECTION SALOON

Mark 1. Short frames. Non-gangwayed. Observation windows at each end. The interior layout consists of two saloons interspersed by a central lavatory/kitchen/guards/luggage section. 90 mph. ETS x.

BR Wagon Lot No. 3095 Swindon 1957. B4 bogies. 30.5 t.

| 999506 | | **M** | WC | *WC* | CS | |

4. PULLMAN CAR COMPANY SERIES

Pullman cars have never generally been numbered as such, although many have carried numbers, instead they have carried titles. However, a scheme of schedule numbers exists which generally lists cars in chronological order. In this section those numbers are shown followed by the car's title. Cars described as "kitchen" contain a kitchen in addition to passenger accommodation and have gas cooking unless otherwise stated. Cars described as "parlour" consist entirely of passenger accommodation. Cars described as "brake" contain a compartment for the use of the guard and a luggage compartment in addition to passenger accommodation.

PULLMAN PARLOUR FIRST

Built 1927 by Midland Carriage & Wagon Company. 26/– 2T. Gresley bogies. 41 t. ETS 2.

213	MINERVA	**PC**	BE	*BP*	SL

PULLMAN KITCHEN FIRST

Built 1928 by Metropolitan Carriage & Wagon Company. 20/– 1T. Gresley bogies. 42 t. ETS 4.

238	PHYLISS	**PC**	BE		SL

PULLMAN PARLOUR FIRST

Built 1928 by Metropolitan Carriage & Wagon Company. 24/– 2T. Gresley bogies. 40 t. ETS 4.

239	AGATHA	**PC**	BE		SL
243	LUCILLE	**PC**	BE	*BP*	SL

PULLMAN KITCHEN FIRST

Built 1925 by BRCW. Rebuilt by Midland Carriage & Wagon Company 1928. 20/– 1T. Gresley bogies. 41 t. ETS 4.

245	IBIS	**PC**	BE	*BP*	SL

PULLMAN PARLOUR FIRST

Built 1928 by Metropolitan Carriage & Wagon Company. 24/– 2T. Gresley bogies. ETS 4.

254	ZENA	**PC**	BE	*BP*	SL

PULLMAN KITCHEN FIRST

Built 1928 by Metropolitan Carriage & Wagon Company. 20/– 1T. Gresley bogies. 42 t. ETS 4.

255	IONE	**PC**	BE	*BP*	SL

PULLMAN KITCHEN COMPOSITE

Built 1932 by Metropolitan Carriage & Wagon Company. Originally included in 6-Pul EMU. Electric cooking. 12/16 1T. EMU bogies. ETS x.

264	RUTH	**PC**	BE		SL

PULLMAN KITCHEN FIRST

Built 1932 by Metropolitan Carriage & Wagon Company. Originally included in "Brighton Belle" EMUs but now used as hauled stock. Electric cooking. 20/– 1T. B5 (SR) bogies (§ EMU bogies). 44 t. ETS 2.

280	AUDREY		**PC**	BE	*BP*	SL
281	GWEN		**PC**	BE	*BP*	SL
283	MONA	§	**PC**	BE		SL
284	VERA		**PC**	BE	*BP*	SL

PULLMAN PARLOUR THIRD

Built 1932 by Metropolitan Carriage & Wagon Company. Originally included in "Brighton Belle" EMUs. –/56 2T. EMU bogies. ETS x.

Non-standard livery: BR Revised Pullman (blue & white lined out in white).

286	CAR No. 86	**O**	BE		SL

PULLMAN BRAKE THIRD

Built 1932 by Metropolitan Carriage & Wagon Company. Originally driving motor cars in "Brighton Belle" EMUs. Traction and control equipment removed for use as hauled stock. –/48 1T. EMU bogies. ETS x.

292	CAR No. 92	**PC**	BE		SL
293	CAR No. 93	**PC**	BE		SL

PULLMAN PARLOUR FIRST

Built 1951 by Birmingham Railway Carriage & Wagon Company. 32/– 2T. Gresley bogies. 39 t. ETS 3.

301	PERSEUS	**PC**	BE	*BP*	SL

Built 1952 by Pullman Car Company, Preston Park using underframe and bogies from 176 RAINBOW, the body of which had been destroyed by fire. 26/– 2T. Gresley bogies. 38 t. ETS 4.

302	PHOENIX	**PC**	BE	*BP*	SL

PULLMAN PARLOUR FIRST

Built 1951 by Birmingham Railway Carriage & Wagon Company. 32/– 2T. Gresley bogies. 39 t. ETS 3.

308	CYGNUS	**PC**	BE	*BP*	SL

PULLMAN BAR FIRST

Built 1951 by Birmingham Railway Carriage & Wagon Company. Rebuilt 1999 by Blake Fabrications, Edinburgh with original timber-framed body replaced by a new fabricated steel body. Contains kitchen, bar, dining saloon and coupé. Electric cooking. 14/– 1T. Gresley bogies. ETS 3.

| 310 | PEGASUS | x | **PC** | LS | *LS* | CL |

Also carries "THE TRIANON BAR" branding.

PULLMAN KITCHEN FIRST

Built 1960 by Birmingham Railway Carriage & Wagon Company. Originally part of the National Collection. Rebuilt by Vintage Trains and returned to service 2021. Electric cooking. 26/– 1T. Commonwealth bogies. ETS x.

| 311 | EAGLE | x | **PC** | VT | *VT* | TM |

PULLMAN PARLOUR FIRST

Built 1960–61 by Metro-Cammell for East Coast Main Line services. –/36 2T. Commonwealth bogies. 38.5 t. ETS x.

| 325 | AMBER | x | **PC** | WC | *WC* | CS |
| 326 | EMERALD | x | **PC** | WC | *WC* | CS |

PULLMAN KITCHEN SECOND

Built 1960–61 by Metro-Cammell for East Coast Main Line services. Commonwealth bogies. –/30 1T. 40 t. ETS x.

| 335 | CAR No. 335 | x | **PC** | VT | *VT* | TM |

PULLMAN PARLOUR SECOND

Built 1960–61 by Metro-Cammell for East Coast Main Line services. 347 is used as an Open First. –/42 2T. Commonwealth bogies. 38.5 t. ETS x.

347	CAR No. 347	x	**M**	WC	*WC*	CS
348	TOPAZ	x	**PC**	WC	*WC*	CS
349	CAR No. 349	x	**PC**	VT	*VT*	TM
350	TANZANITE	x	**PC**	WC	*WC*	CS
351	SAPPHIRE	x	**PC**	WC	*WC*	CS
352	AMETHYST	x	**PC**	WC	*WC*	CS
353	CAR No. 353	x	**PC**	VT		TM

PULLMAN SECOND BAR

Built 1960–61 by Metro-Cammell for East Coast Main Line services. –/24+17 bar seats. Commonwealth bogies. 38.5 t. ETS x.

| 354 | THE HADRIAN BAR | x | **PC** | WC | *WC* | CS |

5. LOCOMOTIVE SUPPORT CARRIAGES

These carriages have been adapted from Mark 1s and Mark 2s for use as support carriages for heritage steam and diesel locomotives. Some seating is retained for the use of personnel supporting the locomotives operation with the remainder of the carriage adapted for storage, workshop, dormitory and catering purposes. These carriages can spend considerable periods of time off the national railway system when the locomotives they support are not being used on that system. No owner or operator details are included in this section. After the depot code, the locomotive(s) each carriage is usually used to support is given.

CORRIDOR BRAKE FIRST

Mark 1. Commonwealth bogies. ETS 2.

4007. Lot No. 30382 Swindon 1959. 35 t.
7025. Lot No. 30718 Swindon 1963. Metal window frames. 36 t.

4007	(14007, 17007)	x	**M**	NY	LNER 61264
7025	(14025)	v	**M**	CS	LMS 45690

CORRIDOR BRAKE FIRST

Mark 2A. Pressure ventilated. B4 bogies. ETS 4.

4060. Lot No. 30775 Derby 1967–68. 32 t.
7096. Lot No. 30786 Derby 1968. 32 t.

4060	(14060, 17060)	v	**M**	TM	LMS 45596	
7096	(14096)		**PC**	SL	SR 35028	MERCATOR

CORRIDOR BRAKE COMPOSITE

Mark 1. ETS 2.

1096. Lot No. 30185 Metro-Cammell 1956. BR Mark 1 bogies. 32.5 t.
1232. Lot No. 30574 GRCW 1960. B4 bogies. 34 t.
1249. Lot No. 30669 Swindon 1961–62. Commonwealth bogies. 36 t.

1096	x	**M**	NY	LNER 60007
1232	x	**M**	SK	LMS 46201
1249	x	**M**	SL	New Build 60163

CORRIDOR BRAKE STANDARD

Mark 1. Metal window frames and melamine interior panelling. ETS 2.

35317/322. Lot No. 30699 Wolverton 1962–63. Commonwealth bogies. 37 t
35451–486. Lot No. 30721 Wolverton 1963. Commonwealth bogies. 37 t.

35317	x	**CC**	CL	Locomotives Services Crewe-based locomotives
35322	x	**M**	CS	WCRC Carnforth-based locomotives
35451	x	**CC**	CL	Locomotives Services Crewe-based locomotives
35461	x	**CH**	CL	GWR 5029
35463	v	**M**	CS	WCRC Carnforth-based locomotives
35468	x	**M**	YK	National Railway Museum locomotives
35470	v	**CH**	TM	Tyseley Locomotive Works-based locos
35476	x	**M**	SK	LMS 46233
35479	v	**M**	SH	LNER 61306
35486	x	**M**	BQ	*Currently not in service*

CORRIDOR BRAKE FIRST

Mark 2C. Pressure ventilated. Renumbered when declassified. B4 bogies
ETS 4.

Lot No. 30796 Derby 1969–70. 32.5 t.

35508 (14128, 17128)	**M**	BQ	LMS 44871/45212/45407

CORRIDOR BRAKE FIRST

Mark 2A. Pressure ventilated. Renumbered when declassified. B4 bogies
ETS 4.

Lot No. 30786 Derby 1968. 32 t.

35517 (14088, 17088)	b	**M**	BQ	LMS 44871/45212/45407
35518 (14097, 17097)	b	**G**	CS	SR 34067

COURIER VEHICLE

Mark 1. Converted 1986–87 from Corridor Brake Standards. ETS 2.

80204/217. Lot No. 30699 Wolverton 1962. Commonwealth bogies. 37 t.
80220. Lot No. 30573 Gloucester 1960. B4 bogies. 33 t.

80204 (35297)	**M**	CS	WCRC Carnforth-based locomotives
80217 (35299)	**M**	CS	WCRC Carnforth-based locomotives
80220 (35276)	**M**	NY	LNER 62005

6. 95xxx & 99xxx RANGE NUMBER CONVERSION TABLE

The following table is presented to help readers identify carriages which may still carry numbers in the 95xxx and 99xxx number ranges of the former private owner number series, which is no longer in general use.

xxxx	BR No.	9xxxx	BR No.	9xxxx	BR No.
5402	Pullman 326	99349	Pullman 349	99673	550
5403	Pullman 311	99350	Pullman 350	99674	551
9025	Pullman 325	99351	Pullman 351	99675	552
9035	35322	99352	Pullman 352	99676	553
9040	21232	99353	Pullman 353	99677	586
9041	35476	99354	Pullman 354	99678	504
9052	Saloon 41	99361	Pullman 335	99679	506
9121	3105	99371	3128	99680	17102
9122	3106	99405	35486	99710	18767
9125	3113	99530	Pullman 301	99716 *	18808
9127	3117	99531	Pullman 302	99718	18862
9128	3130	99532	Pullman 308	99721	18756
9131	Saloon 1999	99534	Pullman 245	99723	35459
9241	35449	99535	Pullman 213	99880	Saloon 159
9302	13323	99536	Pullman 254	99881	Saloon 807
9304	21256	99537	Pullman 280	99883	2108
9311	1882	99539	Pullman 255	99885	2110
9312	35463	99541	Pullman 243	99887	2127
9319	17168	99543	Pullman 284	99953	35468
9326	4954	99546	Pullman 281	99966	34525
9327	5044	99547	Pullman 292	99970	Pullman 232
9328	5033	99548	Pullman 293	99972	Pullman 318
9329	4931	99670	546	99973	324
9347	Pullman 347	99671	548	99974	Pullman 328
9348	Pullman 348	99672	549		

The number 99716 has also been applied to 3416 for filming purposes.

7. SET FORMATIONS

LNER MARK 4 SET FORMATIONS

The LNER Mark 4 sets generally run in fixed formations. Class 91 locomotive are positioned next to Coach B. Most Mark 4 sets were withdrawn in 2019 20, leaving just seven rakes still on lease to LNER. An eighth rake is bein returned to service.

Set	B	C	D	E	F	H	K	L	M	DVT
NL06	12208	12406	12420	12422	12313	10309	11279	11306	11406	82208
NL08	12205	12481	12485	12407	12328	10300	11229	11308	11408	82211
NL12	12212	12431	12404	12426	12330	10333	11284	11312	11412	82212
NL13	12228	12469	12430	12424	12311	10313	11285	11313	11413	82213
NL15	12226	12442	12409	12515	12309	10306	11286	11315	11415	82214
NL16*	12213	12428	12433	12467	12312	10315	11418	11318	11416	82222
NL17	12223	12444	12427	12432	12303	10324	11288	11317	11417	82225
NL26	12220	12474	12465	12429	12325	10311	11295	11326	11426	82223
Spare	12202									82205
Spare	12214									82215

* Set being prepared for returning to service. Formation subject to confirmatio

TfW MARK 4 SET FORMATIONS

In 2021 Transport for Wales returned three shortened four-coach Mark sets to service to replace its Mark 3 sets. They are used on selected service on the Cardiff–Holyhead route, hauled by Class 67s. They are planned to b lengthened to five-coach sets using the spare Open Standard (Disabled coaches listed.

Transport for Wales has also purchased the sets previously planned to b operated by Grand Central and it plans to return these to service by lat 2021 on the Manchester–Swansea route.

Set					DVT	
HD01	12225	10325	11323	12454	82226	(ex-BN23)
HD02	12219	10328	11324	12447	82229	(ex-BN24)
HD03	12217	10312	11325	12446	82216	(ex-BN25)
Spare	12304	12315	12324			

Set						DVT	
GC01	12211	12434	12310	10318	11319	82201	(ex-BN19)
GC02	12224	12477	12326	10321	11320	82200	(ex-BN20)
GC03	12222	12461	12323	10330	11321	82227	(ex-BN21)
GC04	12210	12452	12316	10301	11322	82230	(ex-BN22)
Spare	10305	12215	82220				

E MARK 5A SET FORMATIONS

e entry into service of the new TransPennine Express coaches has been very
tracted. They are used in fixed formations hauled by a Class 68 locomotive
push-pull mode, initially between Liverpool and Scarborough but more
ently largely limited to York–Scarborough. Full service introduction is
nned for 2022.

	E	D	C	B	A
01	11501	12701	12702	12703	12801
02	11502	12704	12705	12706	12814
03	11503	12707	12708	12709	12803
04	11504	12710	12711	12712	12804
05	11505	12713	12714	12715	12805
06	11506	12716	12717	12718	12806
07	11507	12719	12720	12721	12807
08	11508	12722	12723	12724	12808
09	11509	12725	12726	12727	12809
10	11510	12728	12729	12730	12810
11	11511	12731	12732	12733	12811
12	11512	12734	12735	12736	12812
13	11513	12737	12738	12739	12813
are					12802

8. SERVICE STOCK

Carriages in this section are used for internal purposes within the railw
industry, ie they do not generate revenue from outside the industry. M(
are numbered in the former BR departmental number series.

BARRIER, ESCORT & TRANSLATOR VEHICLES

These vehicles are used to move multiple units, HST and other vehic
around the national railway system.

Barrier Vehicles. Mark 1/2A. Renumbered from BR departmental series,
converted from various types. B4 bogies (* Commonwealth bogies).

6330. Mark 2A. Lot No. 30786 Derby 1968.
6336/38/44. Mark 1. Lot No. 30715 Gloucester 1962.
6340. Mark 1. Lot No. 30669 Swindon 1962.
6346. Mark 2A. Lot No. 30777 Derby 1967.
6348. Mark 1. Lot No. 30163 Pressed Steel 1957.

6330	(14084, 975629)	**RO**	A	*RO*	LR
6336	(81591, 92185)	**FB**	A	*GW*	LA
6338	(81581, 92180)	**FB**	A	*RO*	LR
6340	(21251, 975678) *	**RO**	A	*RO*	LR
6344	(81263, 92080)	**RO**	A	*RO*	LR
6346	(9422)	**RO**	A	*RO*	LR
6348	(81233, 92963)	**FB**	A	*GW*	LA

Mark 4 Barrier Vehicles. Mark 2A. Converted from Corridor First. B4 bog
Lot No. 30774 Derby 1968.

6352	(13465, 19465)	**HB**	E		WS
6353	(13478, 19478)	**HB**	E		WS

EMU Translator Vehicles. Mark 1. Converted 1980 from Restaur
Unclassified Opens. 6376/77 have Tightlock couplers and 6378/79 Dell
couplers. Commonwealth bogies.

Lot No. 30647 Wolverton 1959–61.

6376	(1021, 975973)	**PB**	P	*GB*	ZG *(works with 6377*
6377	(1042, 975975)	**PB**	P	*GB*	ZG *(works with 6376*
6378	(1054, 975971)	**RO**	RO	*RO*	LR *(works with 6379*
6379	(1059, 975972)	**RO**	RO	*RO*	LR *(works with 6378*

Brake Force Runners. Mark 1. Previously used as HST Barrier Vehic
Converted from Gangwayed Brake Vans in 1994–95. B4 bogies.

6392. Lot No. 30715 Gloucester 1962.
6397. Lot No. 30716 Gloucester 1962.

6392	(81588, 92183)	**PB**	CS	*CS*	ZA
6397	(81600, 92190)	**PB**	CS	*CS*	ZA

HST Barrier Vehicles. Mark 1. Converted from Gangwayed Brake Vans in 1994–95. B4 bogies.

6393. Lot No. 30716 Gloucester 1962.
6394. Lot No. 30162 Pressed Steel 1956–57.
6398/99. Lot No. 30400 Pressed Steel 1957–58.

6393	(81609, 92196)	**PB**	P	*GB*	ZG
6394	(80878, 92906)	**PB**	P	*GB*	ZG
6398	(81471, 92126)	**PB**	EM	*EM*	NL
6399	(81367, 92994)	**PB**	EM	*EM*	NL

Escort Coaches. Converted from Mark 2A (* Mark 2E) Open Brake Standards. 9419/28 use the same bodyshell as the Mark 2A Corridor Brake First. B4 bogies.

9419. Lot No.30777 Derby 1970.
9428. Lot No.30820 Derby 1970.
9506/08. Lot No.30838 Derby 1972.

9419		**DS**	DR	*DR*	KM
9428		**DS**	DR	*DR*	KM
9506	*	**DS**	DR	*DR*	KM
9508	*	**DS**	DR	*DR*	KM

EMU Translator Vehicles. Converted from Class 508 driving cars.

64664. Lot No. 30979 York 1979–80.
64707. Lot No. 30981 York 1979–80.

64664	**AG**	A	*GB*	ZG	Liwet	*(works with 64707)*
64707	**AG**	A	*GB*	ZG	Labezerin	*(works with 64664)*

EMU Translator Vehicles. Converted from Class 489 DMLVs that had originally been Class 414/3 DMBSOs. Previously used as de-icing coaches.

Lot No. 30452 Ashford/Eastleigh 1959. Mk 4 bogies.

68501	(61281)	**AG**	AF	*RO*	LR
68504	(61286)	**AG**	AF	*RO*	LR

Generator Vans. Former Nightstar Generator Vans converted from Mark 3A Sleeping Cars that are now used as carriage pre-heaters. Gangways removed. Two Cummins diesel generator groups provide a 1500 V train supply.

Lot No. 30960 Derby 1981–83. BT10 bogies.

96371	(10545, 6371)	**EP**	ER		PO
96374	(10585, 6374)	**IC**	ER		YA

Eurostar Barrier Vehicles. Mark 1. Converted from General Utility Vans with bodies removed. Fitted with B4 bogies for use as Eurostar barrier vehicles.

96380/381. Lot No. 30417 Pressed Steel 1958–59.
96383. Lot No. 30565 Pressed Steel 1959.
96384. Lot No. 30616 Pressed Steel 1959–60.

96380	(86386, 6380)	**B**	EU	*EU*	TI
96381	(86187, 6381)	**B**	EU	*EU*	TI
96383	(86664, 6383)	**B**	EU	*EU*	TI
96384	(86955, 6384)	**B**	EU	*EU*	TI

Brake Force Runners. Converted from Motorail vans built 1998–99 by Marcroft Engineering using underframe and running gear from Motorail General Utility Vans. B5 bogies.

Lot No. 30417 Pressed Steel 1958–59.

96604	(86337, 96156)	**Y**	CS	*CS*	ZA
96606	(86324, 96213)	**Y**	CS	*CS*	ZA
96608	(86385, 96216)	**Y**	CS	*CS*	ZA
96609	(86327, 96217)	**Y**	CS	*CS*	ZA

EMU Translator Vehicles. Converted from various Mark 1s.

Non-standard livery: All over blue.

975864. Lot No. 30054 Eastleigh 1951–54. Commonwealth bogies.
975867. Lot No. 30014 York 1950–51. Commonwealth bogies.
975875. Lot No. 30143 Charles Roberts 1954–55. Commonwealth bogies.
975974/978. Lot No. 30647 Wolverton 1959–61. B4 bogies.
977087. Lot No. 30229 Metro–Cammell 1955–57. Commonwealth bogies.

975864	(3849)	**HB**	E		BU		*(works with 975867)*
975867	(1006)	**HB**	E		BU		*(works with 975864)*
975875	(34643)	**O**	E	RO	LR		*(works with 977087)*
975974	(1030)	**AG**	A	GB	ZG	Paschar	*(works with 975978)*
975978	(1025)	**AG**	A	GB	ZG	Perpetiel	*(works with 975974)*
977087	(34971)	**O**	E	RO	LR		*(works with 975875)*

LABORATORY, TESTING & INSPECTION COACHES

These coaches are used for research, testing and inspection on the national railway system. Many are fitted with sophisticated technical equipment.

Plain Line Pattern Recognition Coaches. Converted from BR Mark 2F Buffet First (*) or Open Standard. B4 bogies.

1256. Lot No. 30845 Derby 1973.
5981. Lot No. 30860 Derby 1973–74.

1256	(3296)	*	**Y**	NR	*CS*	ZA
5981			**Y**	NR	*CS*	ZA

Generator Vans. Mark 1. Converted from BR Mark 1 Gangwayed Brake Vans. B5 bogies.

6260. Lot No. 30400 Pressed Steel 1957–58.
6261. Lot No. 30323 Pressed Steel 1957.
6262. Lot No. 30228 Metro–Cammell 1957–58.
6263. Lot No. 30163 Pressed Steel 1957.
6264. Lot No. 30173 York 1956.

6260	(81450, 92116)	**Y**	NR	*CS*	ZA
6261	(81284, 92988)	**Y**	NR	*CS*	ZA
6262	(81064, 92928)	**Y**	NR	*CS*	ZA
6263	(81231, 92961)	**Y**	NR	*CS*	ZA
6264	(80971, 92923)	**Y**	NR	*CS*	ZA

Staff Coach. Mark 2D. Converted from BR Mark 2D Open Brake Standard. Lot No. 30824 Derby 1971. B4 bogies.

9481	**Y**	NR	*CS*	ZA

Test Train Brake Force Runners. Mark 2F. Converted from BR Mark 2F Open Brake Standard. Lot No. 30861 Derby 1974. B4 bogies.

9516	**Y**	NR	*CS*	ZA *(works with 72616)*
9523	**Y**	NR	*CS*	ZA

Driving Trailer Coaches. Converted 2008 at Serco, Derby from Mark 2F Driving Open Brake Standards. Fitted with generator. Disc brakes. B4 bogies.

9701–08. Lot No. 30861 Derby 1974. Converted to Driving Open Brake Standard Glasgow 1974.
9714. Lot No. 30861 Derby 1974. Converted to Driving Open Brake Standard Glasgow 1986.

9701	(9528)	**Y**	NR	*CS*	ZA
9702	(9510)	**Y**	NR	*CS*	ZA
9703	(9517)	**Y**	NR	*CS*	ZA
9708	(9530)	**Y**	NR	*CS*	ZA
9714	(9536)	**Y**	NR	*CS*	ZA

Test Train Brake Coaches. Former Caledonian Sleeper coaches now used for staff accommodation in test trains. Fitted with toilets with retention tanks. Converted from Mark 2E Open Standard with new seating by Railcare Wolverton. B4 bogies.

9801/03. Lot No. 30837 Derby 1972.
9806–10. Lot No. 30844 Derby 1972–73.

9801	(5760)	**FB**	ER	*CS*	ZA
9803	(5799)	**FB**	ER	*CS*	ZA
9806	(5840)	**FB**	ER	*CS*	ZA
9808	(5871)	**FB**	ER	*CS*	ZA
9810	(5892)	**FB**	ER	*CS*	ZA

Ultrasonic Test Coach. Converted from Class 421 EMU MBSO.

62287. Lot No. 30808. York 1970. SR Mark 6 bogies.
62384. Lot No. 30816. York 1970. SR Mark 6 bogies.

62287	**Y**	NR	*CS*	ZA
62384	**Y**	NR	*CS*	ZA

Test Train Brake Force Runners. Converted from Mark 2F Open Standard converted to Class 488/3 EMU TSOLH. These vehicles are included in test trains to provide brake force and are not used for any other purposes. Lot No. 30860 Derby 1973–74. B4 bogies.

72612	(6156)	**Y**	NR	*CS*	ZA
72616	(6007)	**Y**	NR	*CS*	ZA *(works with 9516)*

Structure Gauging Train Coach. Converted from Mark 2F Open Standard converted to Class 488/3 EMU TSOLH. Lot No. 30860 Derby 1973–74. B4 bogies.

72630	(6094)	**Y**	NR	*CS*	ZA *(works with 99666)*

Plain Line Pattern Recognition Coaches. Converted from BR Mark 2F Open Standard converted to Class 488/3 EMU TSOLH. Lot No. 30860 Derby 1973–74. B4 bogies.

72631 (6096)	Y	NR	*CS*	ZA
72639 (6070)	Y	NR	*CS*	ZA

Driving Trailer Coaches. Converted from Mark 3B 110 mph Driving Brake Vans. Fitted with diesel generator. Lot No. 31042 Derby 1988. T4 bogies.

82111	Y	NR	LM
82124	Y	NR	LM
82129	Y	NR	LM
82145	Y	NR	LM

Structure Gauging Train Coach. Converted from BR Mark 2E Open First then converted to exhibition van. Lot No. 30843 Derby 1972–73. B4 bogies.

99666 (3250)	Y	NR	*CS*	ZA	*(works with 72630)*

Inspection Saloon. Converted from Class 202 DEMU TRB at Stewarts Lane for use as a BR Southern Region General Manager's Saloon. Overhauled at FM Rail, Derby 2004–05 for use as a New Trains Project Saloon. Can be used in push-pull mode with suitably equipped locomotives. Eastleigh 1958. SR Mark 4 bogies.

975025 (60755)	G	NR	*CS*	ZA	CAROLINE

Overhead Line Equipment Test Coach ("MENTOR"). Converted from BR Mark 1 Corridor Brake Standard. Lot No. 30142 Gloucester 1954–55. Fitted with pantograph. B4 bogies.

975091 (34615)	Y	NR	*CS*	ZA

New Measurement Train Conference Coach. Converted from prototype HST TF Lot No. 30848 Derby 1972. BT10 bogies.

975814 (11000, 41000)	Y	NR	*CS*	ZA

New Measurement Train Lecture Coach. Converted from prototype HST catering vehicle. Lot No. 30849 Derby 1972–73. BT10 bogies.

975984 (10000, 40000)	Y	NR	*CS*	ZA

Radio Survey Coach. Converted from BR Mark 2E Open Standard. Lot No. 30844 Derby 1972–73. B4 bogies.

977868 (5846)	Y	NR	*CS*	ZA

Staff Coach. Converted from Royal Household couchette Lot No. 30889, which in turn had been converted from BR Mark 2B Corridor Brake First. Lot No. 30790 Derby 1969. B5 bogies.

977969 (14112, 2906)	Y	NR	*CS*	ZA

Track Inspection Train Coach. Converted from BR Mark 2E Open Standard. Lot No. 30844 Derby 1972–73. B4 bogies.

977974 (5854)	Y	NR	*CS*	ZA

ectrification Measurement Coach. Converted from BR Mark 2F Open st converted to Class 488/2 EMU TFOH. Lot No. 30859 Derby 1973–74. bogies.

| 7983 | (3407, 72503) | Y | NR | *CS* | ZA |

w Measurement Train Staff Coach. Converted from HST catering hicle. Lot No. 30884 Derby 1976–77. BT10 bogies.

| 7984 | (40501) | Y | P | *CS* | ZA |

ructure Gauging Train Coaches. Converted from Mark 2F Open andard converted to Class 488/3 EMU TSOLH or from BR Mark 2D Open st subsequently declassified to Open Standard and then converted to hibition van. B4 bogies.

7985. Lot No. 30860 Derby 1973–74.
7986. Lot No. 30821 Derby 1971.

| 7985 | (6019, 72715) | Y | NR | *CS* | ZA *(works with 977986)* |
| 7986 | (3189, 99664) | Y | NR | *CS* | ZA *(works with 977985)* |

w Measurement Train Test Coach. Converted from HST TGS. Lot No. 949 Derby 1982. BT10 bogies.

| 7993 | (44053) | Y | P | *CS* | ZA |

w Measurement Train Track Recording Coach. Converted from HST iS. Lot No. 30949 Derby 1982. BT10 bogies.

| 7994 | (44087) | Y | P | *CS* | ZA |

w Measurement Train Coach. Converted from HST catering vehicle. Lot . 30921 Derby 1978–79. Fitted with generator. BT10 bogies.

| 7995 | (40719, 40619) | Y | P | *CS* | ZA |

dio Survey Coach. Converted from Mark 2F Open Standard converted to ass 488/3 EMU TSOLH. Lot No. 30860 Derby 1973–74. B4 bogies.

| 7997 | (72613, 6126) | Y | NR | *CS* | ZA |

ack Recording Coach. Purpose built Mark 2. BR Wagon Lot No. 3830 rby 1976. B4 bogies.

| 9550 | | Y | NR | *CS* | ZA |

trasonic Test Coaches. Converted from Class 421 EMU MBSO and Class 2 EMU MSO.

9602/605. Lot No. 30862 York 1974. SR Mk 6 bogies.
9606. Lot No. 30816. York 1970. SR Mk 6 bogies.

9602	(62483)	Y	NR	*CS*	ZA
9605	(62482)	Y	NR	*CS*	ZA
9606	(62356)	Y	NR	*CS*	ZA

BREAKDOWN TRAIN COACHES

These coaches are formed in trains used for the recovery of derailed railw
vehicles and were converted from BR Mark 1 Corridor Brake Standard a
General Utility Van. The current use of each vehicle is given.

971001/003/004. Lot No. 30403 York/Glasgow 1958–60. Commonwealth bogi
971002. Lot No. 30417 Pressed Steel 1958–59. Commonwealth bogies.
975087. Lot No. 30032 Wolverton 1951–52. BR Mark 1 bogies.
975464. Lot No. 30386 Charles Roberts 1956–58. Commonwealth bogies
975471. Lot No. 30095 Wolverton 1953–55. Commonwealth bogies.
975477. Lot No. 30233 GRCW 1955–57. BR Mark 1 bogies.
975486. Lot No. 30025 Wolverton 1950–52. Commonwealth bogies.

971001	(86560, 94150)	**Y**	NR	*DB*	SP	Tool & Generator V
971002	(86624, 94190)	**Y**	NR	*DB*	SP	Tool Van
971003	(86596, 94191)	**Y**	NR	*DB*	SP	Tool Van
971004	(86194, 94168)	**Y**	NR	*DB*	SP	Tool Van
975087	(34289)	**Y**	NR	*DB*	SP	Tool & Generator V
975464	(35171)	**Y**	NR	*DB*	SP	Staff Coach
975471	(34543)	**Y**	NR	*DB*	SP	Staff Coach
975477	(35108)	**Y**	NR	*DB*	SP	Staff Coach
975486	(34100)	**Y**	NR	*DB*	SP	Tool & Generator V

INFRASTRUCTURE MAINTENANCE COACH

Winterisation Train Coach. Converted from BR Mark 2E Open Standard. L
No. 30844 Derby 1972–73. B4 bogies.

977869	(5858)	**Y**	NR	*DR*	Perth CS

INTERNAL USER VEHICLES

These vehicles are confined to yards and depots or do not normally move.
Details are given of the internal user number (if allocated), type, former
identity, current use and location. Many no longer see regular use.

* = Grounded body.

041989*	BR SPV 975423	Stores Van	Toton Depot
061202*	BR GUV 93498	Stores Van	Laira Depot, Plymouth
	BR NKA 94199	Stores Van	EG Steels, Hamilton
	BR NA 94322*	Stores Van	WCRC, Carnforth Depot
083602	BR CCT 94494	Stores Van	Three Bridges Station
	BR NB 94548*	Stores van	WCRC, Carnforth Depot
083637	BR NW 99203	Stores van	Stewarts Lane Depot
083644	BR Ferry Van 889201	Stores van	Eastleigh Depot
083664	BR Ferry Van 889203	Stores van	Eastleigh Depot
–	BR Open Standard 5636	Instruction Coach	St Philip's Marsh Depot
–	BR BV 6396	Stores van	Longsight Depot (Manchester)
–	BR RFKB 10256	Instruction Coach	Yoker Depot
–	BR RFKB 10260	Instruction Coach	Yoker Depot
–	BR SPV 88045*	Stores Van	Thames Haven Yard
–	BR NL 94003	Stores Van	Burton-upon-Trent Depot
–	BR NK 94121	Stores Van	Toton Depot
–	BR NB 94438	Stores Van	Toton Depot
–	BR CCT 94663*	Stores Van	Mossend Up Yard
–	BR GUV 96139	Stores van	Longsight Depot, Manchester
–	BR Ferry Van 889200	Stores van	Stewarts Lane Depot
–	BR Ferry Van 889202	Stores van	Stewarts Lane Depot
–	SR PMV 977045*	Stores Van	EMD, Longport Works
–	SR CCT 2516*	Stores Van	Eastleigh Depot

Abbreviations:

BV =	Barrier Vehicle
CCT =	Covered Carriage Truck (a 4-wheeled van similar to a GUV)
GUV =	General Utility Van (bogied van with side and end doors)
NAA =	Propelling Control Vehicle
NB =	High Security Brake Van (converted from Gangwayed Brake Van, gangways removed)
NK =	High Security General Utility Van (end doors removed)
NKA =	High Security Mail Van
NL =	Newspaper Van (converted from a GUV)
NW =	Bullion Van (converted from a Corridor Brake Standard)
PMV =	Parcels & Miscellaneous Van (a 4-wheeled van similar to a CCT but without end doors)
RFKB =	Kitchen Buffet First
SPV =	Special Parcels Van (a 4-wheeled van converted from a Fish Van)

9. COACHING STOCK AWAITING DISPOSAL

This list shows the locations of carriages awaiting disposal. The definition of which vehicles are awaiting disposal is somewhat vague, but often these are vehicles of types not now in normal service, those not expected to see further use or that have originated from preservationists as a source of spares or possible future use or carriages which have been damaged by fire, vandalism or collision.

1201	TM	3379	DE	5888	SH	9529	WS
1252	SH	3388	FA	5922	WS	9531	WS
1253	SH	3399	FA	5924	WS	10242	BU
1258	CS	3400	BU	5925	SH	10245	CS
1644	CS	3408	CS	5928	TM	10530	ZN
1650	CS	3416	TM	5943	CS	10578	ZN
1652	CS	3417	DE	5954	BU	10588	ZN
1655	CS	3424	BU	5958	SH	10656	ZN
1658	CL	4362	BU	5959	WS	11006	BU
1663	CS	4796	BU	5978	SH	11021	LM
1670	CS	4799	BU	6009	SH	11028	ZB
1679	RO	4849	CS	6029	SH	11097	BU
1696	YA	4860	CS	6036	WS	12096	ZN
1800	SH	4932	CS	6041	CS	13323	CS
1883	CL	4997	CS	6045	SH	13508	RO
1954	CL	5027	CS	6050	CS	17013	ZG
2108	CS	5054	RO	6073	SH	17168	CS
2110	CS	5179	TM	6110	BU	18767	SH
2127	CS	5183	TM	6134	SH	18808	SH
2131	CS	5186	TM	6139	BU	18862	CS
2833	CS	5194	TM	6151	SH	21268	RO
2909	CS	5331	FA	6152	WS	34525	CS
3051	YA	5386	FA	6154	SH	35333	ZG
3060	CL	5420	TM	6175	CS	35467	CL
3091	RO	5453	CS	6179	CS	68505	ZG
3241	CS	5463	CS	6324	CP	80212	CS
3255	FA	5478	CS	6351	BU	80374	BU
3277	RO	5491	CS	6360	NL	80403	CS
3279	BU	5569	CS	6361	NL	80404	CS
3292	BU	5631	BU	6364	CF	80414	SL
3295	RO	5657	BU	6365	CF	82101	LW
3309	TM	5710	ZM	6412	CL	82126	LW
3318	BU	5737	CS	6720	FA	92114	ZA
3331	BU	5740	CS	7204	CL	92159	CS
3334	DE	5756	CS	7931	BU	92908	CS
3336	DE	5777	BU	9440	SH	93723	BY
3351	TM	5797	RO	9489	CS	94058	BU
3358	BU	5815	SH	9490	BU	94101	CS
3368	FA	5876	SH	9496	DE	94106	BU

116	BU	94406	CS	94538	CL	96607	Barry
153	WE	94408	CS	94539	CS	99019	CS
166	BU	94410	WE	94540	TJ	99884	YA
170	CL	94420	CS	94542	CS	975081	BU
176	BU	94423	BU	94545	HM	975280	BU
195	BU	94427	WE	94546	HL	975454	TO
196	CS	94428	CS	94547	CS	975484	CS
197	BU	94429	HM	95300	CS	975490	BU
214	CS	94431	CS	95410	CS	975639	CS
222	CS	94434	CL	95727	WE	975681	CS
227	HM	94445	WE	95754	CS	975682	CS
229	CL	94450	WE	95761	WE	975685	CS
302	HL	94451	WE	95763	BU	975686	CS
303	HL	94482	CS	96110	CS	975687	CS
304	MH	94488	BU	96132	CS	975688	CS
306	HL	94490	BU	96135	CS	975920	Portobello
308	CS	94492	WE	96164	CS	977085	BU
310	WE	94495	HL	96165	CS	977095	CS
311	WE	94498	CS	96170	CS	977169	BU
313	WE	94504	HL	96178	CS	977241	BU
323	HL	94512	CS	96182	CS	977450	BU
326	HL	94515	ZG	96191	CS	977618	BY
332	CS	94517	BU	96192	CS	083439	BU
333	HL	94520	BU	96372	LM		
335	CL	94522	CL	96373	LM	DS70220 Western Trading Estate Siding, North Acton	
336	CL	94525	CS	96375	LM		
337	WE	94526	CS	96602	Barry	Pullman 315 CS	
338	WE	94527	HL	96603	CF	Pullman 316 HN	
401	CS	94531	BU	96605	Barry		

10. CODES

10.1. LIVERY CODES

The colour of the lower half of the bodyside is stated first. Minor variatio
to these liveries are ignored.

AG Arlington Fleet Services (green).
AL Advertising/promotional livery (see class heading for details).
AR Anglia Railways (turquoise blue with a white stripe).
AV Arriva Trains (turquoise blue with white doors).
AW Arriva Trains Wales/Welsh Government sponsored dark & light blue
B   BR blue.
BG BR blue & grey lined out in white.
CA Caledonian Sleeper (dark blue).
CC BR Carmine & Cream.
CH BR Western Region/GWR chocolate & cream lined out in gold.
CM Chiltern Railways Mainline (two-tone grey/white & silver with blue stripe
DR Direct Rail Services (dark blue with light blue or dark grey roof).
DS Revised Direct Rail Services (dark blue, light blue & green. Compass log
EA East Midlands Trains revised HST (dark blue, orange & red).
EP European Passenger Services (two-tone grey with dark blue roof).
FB First Group dark blue.
FD First Great Western "Dynamic Lines" (dark blue with thin mu
        coloured lines on lower bodyside).
FS First Group (indigo blue with pink & white stripes).
G   BR Southern Region/SR green.
GA Greater Anglia (white with red doors & black window surrounds).
GW Great Western Railway (TOC) dark green.
HB HSBC Rail (Oxford blue & white)
IC BR InterCity (light grey/red stripe/white stripe/dark grey).
M   BR maroon (maroon lined out in straw & black).
MP Midland Pullman (nanking blue & white).
O   Non-standard (see class heading for details).
PB Porterbrook Leasing Company (blue).
PC Pullman Car Company (umber & cream with gold lettering lined ou
        gold).
RB Riviera Trains Oxford blue.
RC Rail Charter Services (green with a broad silver bodyside stripe).
RP Royal Train (claret, lined out in red & black).
RV Riviera Trains Great Briton (Oxford blue & cream, lined out in gold).
SI ScotRail InterCity (light grey & dark blue with INTER7CITY branding
SR ScotRail – Scotland's Railways (dark blue with Scottish Saltire fla
        white/blue flashes).
ST Stagecoach {long-distance stock} (white & dark blue with dark b
        window surrounds and red & orange swishes at unit ends).
TP TransPennine Express (silver, grey, blue & purple).
V   Virgin Trains (red with black doors extending into bodysides, th
        white lower bodyside stripes).

Virgin Trains East Coast (red & white with black window surrounds).
Northern Belle (crimson lake & cream lined out in gold).
Virgin Trains silver (silver, with black window surrounds, white cantrail stripe and red roof. Red swept down at unit ends).
CrossCountry (two tone silver with deep crimson ends & pink doors).
Network Rail yellow.

0.2. OWNER CODES

e following codes are used to define the ownership details of the rolling ck listed in this book. Codes shown indicate either the legal owner or sponsible custodian" of each vehicle.

Angel Trains
Arlington Fleet Services
Arriva UK Trains
Belmond (UK)
Beacon Rail
Brodie Leasing
Colas Rail
Data Acquisition & Testing Services
DB Cargo (UK)
Direct Rail Services
Eversholt Rail (UK)
Electric Traction Limited
East Midlands Railway
Eastern Rail Services
Eurostar (UK)
First Group
Great Western Railway (assets of the Greater Western franchise)
Lombard Finance
Locomotive Services
London Underground
North Norfolk Railway
Network Rail
North Yorkshire Moors Railway Enterprises
Porterbrook Leasing Company
PMP Events
Other private owner
The Princess Royal Class Locomotive Trust
Rail Operations Group
Rampart Engineering
Riviera Trains
The Scottish Railway Preservation Society
Transport for Wales
Vintage Trains
Wabtec Rail Group
West Coast Railway Company

10.3. OPERATOR CODES

The two letter operator codes give the current operator (by trading name)
This is the organisation which facilitates the use of the coach and may n
be the actual Train Operating Company which runs the train on which th
particular coach is used. If no operator code is shown then the vehicle
not in use at present.

BP	Belmond British Pullman	*NY*	North Yorkshire Moors Railw
CA	Caledonian Sleeper	*RO*	Rail Operations Group
CR	Chiltern Railways	*RS*	The Royal Scotsman (Belmon
CS	Colas Rail	*RT*	Royal Train
DB	DB Cargo (UK)	*RV*	Riviera Trains
DR	Direct Rail Services	*SP*	The Scottish Railway
EM	East Midlands Railway		Preservation Society
EU	Eurostar (UK)	*SR*	ScotRail
GA	Greater Anglia	*TP*	TransPennine Express
GB	GB Railfreight	*TW*	Transport for Wales
GW	Great Western Railway	*VT*	Vintage Trains
LN	London North Eastern Railway	*WC*	West Coast Railway Compan
LS	Locomotive Services	*XC*	CrossCountry

10.4. ALLOCATION & LOCATION CODES

Code	Depot	Depot Operator
AL	Aylesbury	Chiltern Railways
BK	Bristol Barton Hill	Arriva TrainCare
BN	Bounds Green (London)	Hitachi
BO	Bo'ness (West Lothian)	The Bo'ness & Kinneil Railway
BQ	Bury (Greater Manchester)	East Lancashire Railway Trust
BR	MoD Bicester	*Storage location only*
BU	Burton-upon-Trent	Nemesis Rail
BY	Bletchley	West Midlands Trains
CF	Cardiff Canton	Transport for Wales
CL	Crewe LNWR Heritage	LNWR Heritage Company
CN	Castle Donington RFT	*Storage location only*
CP	Crewe Carriage Shed	Arriva TrainCare
CS	Carnforth	West Coast Railway Company
DE	East Dereham (Norfolk)	Mid Norfolk Railway
DR	Doncaster Belmont Yard/RMT	*Storage location only*
DY	Derby Etches Park	East Midlands Railway
EC	Edinburgh Craigentinny	Hitachi
EH	Eastleigh	Arriva TrainCare
EP	Ely Papworth Sidings	*Storage location only*
FA	Fawley (Hampshire)	*Storage location only*
HL	Hellifield	*Storage location only*
HM	Healey Mills (Wakefield)	*Storage location only*
HN	Hamilton (Glasgow)	Assenta Rail

IL	Ilford (London)	Greater Anglia
IS	Inverness	ScotRail
KM	Carlisle Kingmoor	Direct Rail Services
KR	Kidderminster	Severn Valley Railway
LA	Laira (Plymouth)	Great Western Railway
LM	Long Marston Rail Innovation Centre	Porterbrook Leasing
LR	Leicester	UK Rail Leasing
LW	MoD Longtown (Cumbria)	*Storage location only*
MA	Longsight (Manchester)	Alstom
ME	Mossend Yard	*Storage location only*
MH	Millerhill (Edinburgh)	*Storage location only*
NL	Neville Hill (Leeds)	Northern
NO	Weybourne (Norfolk)	North Norfolk Railway
NY	Grosmont (North Yorkshire)	North Yorkshire Moors Railway Enterprises
PM	St Philip's Marsh (Bristol)	Great Western Railway
PO	Polmadie (Glasgow)	Alstom
PZ	Penzance Long Rock	Great Western Railway
RD	Ruddington (Nottingham Heritage Railway)	125 Group
RJ	Rectory Junction (Nottingham)	Data Acquisition & Testing Services
RO	Rowsley (Derbyshire)	Peak Rail
RS	Ruislip (London)	London Underground
SH	Southall (London)	West Coast Railway Co/Locomotive Services
SK	Swanwick West (Derbyshire)	The Princess Royal Locomotive Trust
SL	Stewarts Lane (London)	Govia Thameslink Railway/Belmond
SP	Springs Branch (Wigan)	DB Cargo (UK)
TJ	Tavistock Junction Yard (Plymouth)	*Storage location only*
TI	Temple Mills (London)	Eurostar (UK)
TM	Tyseley Locomotive Works	Vintage Trains
TO	Toton (Nottinghamshire)	DB Cargo (UK)
WB	Wembley (London)	Alstom
WE	Willesden Brent Sidings	*Storage location only*
WO	Wolsingham (Weardale Railway)	RMS Locotec
WS	Worksop (Nottinghamshire)	Harry Needle Railroad Company
YA	Great Yarmouth	Eastern Rail Services
YK	National Railway Museum (York)	National Museum of Science & Industry
ZA	RTC Business Park (Derby)	LORAM (UK)
ZB	Doncaster Works	Wabtec Rail
ZC	Crewe Works	Alstom UK
ZD	Derby Works	Alstom UK
ZG	Eastleigh Works	Arlington Fleet Services
ZI	Ilford Works	Alstom UK
ZJ	Stoke-on-Trent Works	Axiom Rail (Stoke)
ZK	Kilmarnock Caledonia Works	Brodie Engineering
ZM	Kilmarnock Bonnyton Works	Brodie Engineering
ZN	Wolverton Works	Gemini Rail Group
ZR	Holgate Works (York)	Network Rail